AMERICAN VOICES FROM

The Civil Rights Movement

AMERICAN VOICES FROM

The Civil Rights Movement

Elizabeth Sirimarco

MARSHALL CAVENDISH
NEW YORK

FOR ET AND MTM

Benchmark Books
Marshall Cavendish
99 White Plains Road
Tarrytown, New York 10591-9001
www.marshallcavendish.com

Library of Congress Cataloging-in-Publication Data
Sirimarco, Elizabeth, 1966–
The civil rights movement / by Elizabeth Sirimarco.
p. cm. — (American voices from—)
Summary: Presents the history of the civil rights movement in the United States, from Reconstruction to the late 1960s, through excerpts from letters, newspaper articles, speeches, songs, and poems of the time. Includes bibliographical references and index.
ISBN 0-7614-1697-8
1. African Americans—Civil rights—History—Sources—Juvenile literature. 2. Civil rights movements—United States—History—Sources—Juvenile literature. 3. United States—Race relations—Sources—Juvenile literature. [1. African Americans—Civil rights—History—Sources. 2. Civil rights movements—Sources. 3. Race relations—Sources.] I. Title. II. Series.
E185.5.S57 2004   323.1'196073—dc21
2003007952

Printed in China
1 3 5 6 4 2

Series design and composition by Anne Scatto / PIXEL PRESS
Photo research by Linda Sykes Picture Research, Inc., Hilton Head, SC

The photographs in this book are used by permission and through the courtesy of:
Matt Herron/Take Stock: Cover; Private Collection, © Michael Escoffery ARS, NY/Art Resource, NY: ii; Division of Political History/National Museum of American History/Smithsonian Institution, Washington, DC: viii; American Antiquarian Society, Worcester, MA: xi; The Granger Collection, NY: xii, xiv, xvii, xxii, 2, 5, 7, 14, 17, 26, 28, 34; National Portrait Gallery, Smithsonian Institution, Washington/Art Resource, NY: xix; AP/Wide World Photos: xx, 43, 51, 71, 80, 85, 97, 98, 108; Ohio Historical Society: 10; Danny Lyon/Magnum Photos: 12; Library of Congress: 19, 20, 23, 49, 56; Hulton Archive/Getty Images: 31, 101; Annenberg Rare Book & Manuscript Library/University of Pennsylvania: 36; Corbis: 41, 94, 118; National Portrait Gallery, Smithsonian Institution, Washington/Art Resource, NY: 46; Slim Aarons/Hulton/Getty Images: 52; Constantine Manos/Magnum Photos: 61; Burt Glinn/Magnum Photos: 62; Ernst Haas/Hulton/Getty Images: 67; Bob Adelman/Magnum Photos, Inc.: 69, 82; William Lovelace/Hulton/Getty Images: 74, 126; Fred Ward/Black Star: 78; Charles Moore/AP/Wide World Photos: 88; John F. Kennedy Library: 91; Eve Arnold/Magnum Photos: 106, 112; David J. & Janice L. Frent Collection/Corbis: 125

ON THE COVER: The March from Selma, 1965, during the civil rights movement.

ON THE TITLE PAGE: *400 Years of Our People*, by Michael Escoffery, 1994.

Acknowledgments

The author is grateful to the following individuals, publishers, and groups for permission to include previously copyrighted material:

"Southern Exposure," by Josh White. Courtesy of Folk/Blues Music Co./ASCAP. Reprinted with permission.

Ray Sprigle, "A Visit to a Jim Crow School." *Pittsburgh Post-Gazette*, August 1948. Reprinted with permission of the publisher.

The author thanks the National Association for the Advancement of Colored People for authorizing the use of "The Legal Attack to Secure Civil Rights," speech given by Thurgood Marshall, July 13, 1942, at the NAACP Wartime Conference, Chicago, IL.

Excerpt from *I Never Had It Made* reprinted with permission. © Rachel Robinson under license authorized by CMG Worldwide, www.JackieRobinson.com.

"A Bronzeville Mother Loiters in Mississippi, Meanwhile a Mississippi Mother Burns Bacon," by Gwendolyn Brooks, reprinted by consent of Brooks Permissions.

Excerpt from *Voices of Freedom* by Henry Hampton and Steve Fayer, copyright © 1990 by Blackside Inc. Used by permission of Bantam Books, a division of Random House, Inc.

"Integrated Bus Suggestions" from the Inez Jessie Baskin Papers, reprinted with permission from the Alabama Department of Archives and History, Montgomery, Alabama.

Excerpt from *Warriors Don't Cry* by Melba Pattillo Beals reprinted with the permission of Simon & Schuster. Copyright © 1994, 1995 by Melba Pattillo Beals.

Excerpt from *The Tiger* (Central High student newspaper, Little Rock, Arkansas), October 3, 1957, reprinted with permission of the Central High Journalism Department.

Excerpts from "Letter from a Birmingham Jail" and "I Have a Dream" reprinted by arrangement with the Estate of Martin Luther King Jr., c/o Writers House as agent for the proprietor New York, NY. *Copyright 1963 Dr. Martin Luther King Jr., copyright renewed 1991 Coretta Scott King.*

Excerpt from *For Us, the Living* copyright © 1967 Myrlie B. Evers and William Peters. Reprinted by permission of Curtis Brown, Ltd.

"Racial Tension Mounts in Birmingham after Four Killed in Church Bombing," reprinted by permission of the *Montgomery Advertiser.*

"We Shall Overcome": Musical and Lyrical adaptation by Silphia Horton, Frank Hamilton, Guy Carawan, and Pete Seeger. Inspired by African American Gospel Singing, members of the Food & Tobacco Workers Union, Charleston, SC, and the southern Civil Rights Movement. TRO © 1960 (Renewed) and 1963 (Renewed) Ludlow Music, Inc., New York, NY. International Copyright Secured. All Rights Reserved Including Public Performance for Profit.

Roy Reed, "Alabama Police Use Gas and Clubs to Rout Negroes." © 1965 *New York Times.* Reprinted with permission.

Contents

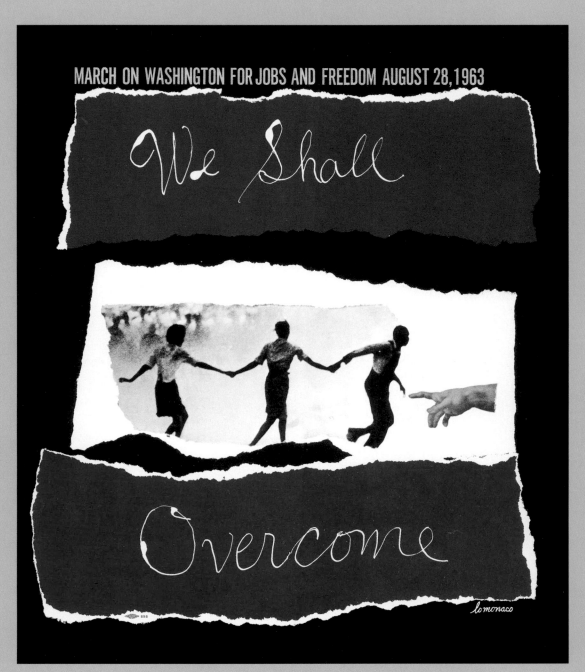

Photographs, paintings, and drawings—like this poster from the March on Washington of 1963—are excellent examples of primary sources. These keys to the past provide a richer, more meaningful look at our history.

About Primary Sources

What Is a Primary Source?

In the pages that follow, you will be hearing many different "voices" from an important period in America's past. Some of the selections are long while others are short. You'll find many easy to understand at first reading, but some may require several readings. All the selections have one thing in common, however. They are primary sources. This is the name historians give to the bits and pieces of information that make up the record of human existence. Primary sources are important to us because they are the very essence, the core material for all historical investigation. You can call them "history" itself.

Primary sources *are* evidence; they give historians the all-important clues they need to understand the past. Perhaps you have read a detective story in which a sleuth has to solve a mystery by piecing together bits of evidence he or she uncovers. The detective makes deductions, or educated guesses based on the evidence, and solves the mystery once all the deductions point in a certain direction. Historians work in much the same way. Like detectives, historians analyze the data by careful reading and rereading. After much analysis, historians draw conclusions about an event, a person, or an entire era. Individual historians may analyze the same evidence and come to different conclusions. This is why there is often sharp disagreement about an event.

Primary sources are also called *documents*—a rather dry word to describe what can be just about anything: an official speech by a government leader, an old map, an act of Congress, a letter worn out from too much handling, an entry hastily scrawled in a diary, a detailed newspaper account of a tragic event, a funny or sad song, a colorful poster, a cartoon, a faded photograph, or someone's eloquent remembrance captured on tape or film.

By examining the following primary sources, you, the reader, will be taking on the role of historian. Here is a chance to immerse yourself in a fascinating era of American history—the civil rights movement. You will come to know the voices of the men and women who lived through this challenging period. You will read the words of the movement's leaders and of ordinary citizens, of activists and journalists, of poets and musicians and protesters.

Some of the sources you will read may be difficult to understand at first. You may encounter some difficult words and concepts or formal language. Don't be discouraged! Trying to figure out language is exactly the kind of work a historian does. Like a historian, when your work is done, you will have a deeper, more meaningful understanding of the past.

How to Read a Primary Source

Each document in this book deals with the civil rights movement. Some of the documents are from government archives such as the presidential libraries. Others are from the writings and speeches of major figures in the movement, such as Ida B. Wells and W. E. B. Du Bois, Thurgood Marshall and Fannie Lou Hamer, Martin Luther King and Malcolm X. Other documents are taken from poetry, memoirs, and newspaper articles. All of the documents, major and minor, help us to understand what it was like to live during the civil rights movement.

As you read each document, ask yourself some basic but important questions. Who is writing? What is the writer's point of view? Who is the writer's audience? What is he or she trying to tell that audience? Is the message clearly expressed or is it implied, that is, stated indirectly? What words does the writer use to convey his or her message? Are the words emotion-

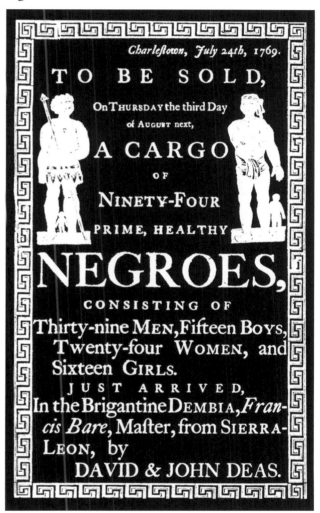

It is not difficult to figure out the purpose of this primary source, a handbill from 1769, only shocking to realize that men, women, and children were actually sold like cattle.

A photograph can capture a moment in history, transporting the viewer to another time and place. This 1939 image shows a man drinking from a segregated water fountain in Oklahoma City, Oklahoma. Examination of this primary source allows us to gain a deeper understanding of what it was like to live in a world divided by race.

filled or objective in tone? If you are looking at a photograph, examine it carefully, taking in all the details. Where do you think it was taken? What's happening in the foreground? In the background? Is it posed? Or is it an action shot? How can you tell? Who do you think took the picture? What is its purpose? These are questions that help you think critically about a document.

Some tools have been included with the documents to help you in your historical investigations. Unusual words have been defined near some selections. Thought-provoking questions follow the documents. They help focus your reading so you get the most out of the document. As you read each selection, you'll probably come up with many questions of your own. That's great! The work of a historian always leads to many, many questions. Some can be answered; others cannot and require further investigation. Perhaps when you finish this book, your questions will lead you to further explorations of the civil rights movement.

African-American men, among them soldiers who fought for the Union, cast their first vote in the South following the Civil War. Exercising their right to vote was just the first step, however, in the long, hard climb for full citizenship. This picture was published in a newspaper in 1867.

Introduction

A CITIZEN'S RIGHTS

The first Africans who came to America left their native lands under circumstances very different from those of other immigrants to the New World. In 1619 a group arrived in Jamestown, Virginia, and over the next 250 years some 600,000 would follow—but not by choice. Torn from their homes and families, they arrived starving, stripped nearly bare, and in chains, thrust into a life of slavery in a strange land. It was not until the mid–nineteenth century, at the end of the American Civil War in 1865, that all the slaves were set free. The injustice—the evil—of slavery had been outlawed, but the future of the former slaves would be one of struggle.

The aftermath of the Civil War thrust the United States into a trying period: the Reconstruction era. United again as a single nation, the North and the South had to find a way to overcome the serious issues that had divided them. One of the most challenging questions was the status of the former slaves. They were now considered U.S. citizens and thus had the same civil rights, or personal freedoms, guaranteed by law to other American citizens. But how to protect these rights in the face of deeply rooted prejudice? During the twelve years of Reconstruction, three amendments to the U.S. Constitution were passed with this purpose in mind.

The new amendments, often called the Civil War amendments, promised freedom and equal rights to all American citizens. The Thirteenth Amendment abolished slavery. The Fourteenth Amendment promised the rights of citizenship to all people born or naturalized in the United States. These rights include, among others, freedom of speech, freedom of religion, and the right to gather peacefully for political or other purposes. The Fourteenth Amendment also prohibited individual states from taking away these rights. Finally, the Fifteenth Amendment granted suffrage—the right to vote—to black men. (Women of all races would not be permitted to vote until 1920.) Once passed, the amendments became federal law and could be enforced by Congress.

To give the federal government more power to protect black citizens, Congress passed the Civil Rights Act of 1875. This legislation was intended to ensure that all African Americans, including former slaves, would have equal access to public facilities. The act promised that "all persons within the jurisdiction of the United States shall be entitled to the full and equal enjoyment of the accommodations, advantages, facilities, and privileges of inns, public conveyances on land or water, theaters, and other places of public amusement; subject only to the conditions and limitations established by law, and applicable alike to citizens of every race and color, regardless of any previous condition of servitude."

Shortly after the Civil War, African Americans dove into the political arena with great zeal. This painting from 1872 depicts the nation's first black senators and representatives.

Congress hoped that the new legislation, along with the Civil War amendments, would be sufficient to secure the rights of black Americans. But it was not to be.

During the early years of Reconstruction, representatives from the North ran governments in the Southern states to ensure that the amendments were not violated. Blacks participated enthusiastically in the democratic process. They exercised their right to vote and held public office at all levels of government, from local councils to the U.S. Congress. But as life returned to normal after the war and Northern representatives left the South, many white

Southerners quickly found ways to resist and defy the law. They made it difficult for blacks to find decent work to support their families. Vigilante groups such as the Ku Klux Klan used violence to keep blacks from voting or participating in politics. State legislatures created laws to sidestep the amendments and the Civil Rights Act. Some states, for example, allowed only landowners or literate people to vote. How many former slaves were fortunate enough to own land? How many had ever learned to read and write when laws had long restricted them from doing so?

Moving to the North offered little more opportunity. Few Northerners truly viewed the former slaves as equal citizens. Working-class whites resented the new arrivals, who they feared would take away their jobs. Policies, official or simply understood, kept blacks from living in white neighborhoods or attending the best schools. Blacks across the nation faced racism and discrimination. They had won freedom, but they lacked opportunity in a country that claimed to be the greatest democracy in the history of the world.

Many Americans consider the civil rights movement to belong to the period in the 1950s and 1960s when black citizens undertook a massive, organized struggle for justice and equality. But the story of civil rights began long before that significant chapter in our history. Those who began the struggle well over a century ago deserve their share of the credit for the great strides made toward equality in the days of Thurgood Marshall and Martin Luther King Jr.

In the chapters that follow, you will learn of milestones in the modern civil rights movement. They include 1954's important

W.E.B. Du Bois, the first African American to earn a doctorate from Harvard University, was one of the most influential early activists.

A hero of the civil rights movement, Rosa Parks was arrested in 1955 for refusing to give up her seat on a bus to a white passenger. Her simple, courageous act of defiance helped ignite the movement.

U.S. Supreme Court decision, *Brown v. the Board of Education*, 1964's passage of the Voting Rights Act, and the 1968 assassination of Martin Luther King, the year many consider to mark the end of the movement. You will also hear the stories of early activists who were the first to take courageous steps on the road to civil rights. You will learn how the burden of racism became too much to bear, how black Americans, grown tired of waiting for change, joined forces in protest. You also will learn about violence and hatred. And you will learn of the prejudice and inequality that dishonored a nation built on the ideals of liberty and democracy.

The story of civil rights in America is not an easy one to recount. It can provoke anger and embarrassment, shock and sorrow. But it can also evoke great pride. The people who struggled for civil rights, at significant personal risk and with tremendous dignity, were, after all, Americans.

Jim Crow, shown on this 1835 sheet-music cover, was a character from minstrel shows. It is unclear how he came to be associated with the system of laws that supported segregation in the South, which were often referred to as Jim Crow.

Chapter I

The Roots of a Movement

THE FEDERAL GOVERNMENT enacted the Civil War amendments and the Civil Rights Act of 1875 to protect the former slaves, but these measures were largely ineffective. As Northerners withdrew from the South after Reconstruction, Southerners created city ordinances and state laws to restrict blacks' rights and their access to both public and private places—from restaurants and libraries to neighborhoods and churches. The system of laws and customs that supported segregation and discrimination across America, especially in the South, became known as Jim Crow. (Jim Crow was a character from minstrel shows, but no one is sure how the name came to be used in this context.) As the nineteenth·century came to a close, it was clear that blacks were considered second-class citizens. The government had not done enough to secure their civil rights, and it would do even less in the coming years.

In 1896 the Supreme Court decided that the Civil Rights Act was unconstitutional; the landmark decision gave official protection to Jim Crow. The Court's justices stated that as long as blacks had "equal" facilities, laws separating the races were perfectly legal.

A black passenger is being evicted from a "whites only" railway car in this nineteenth-century engraving.

This idea became known as the "separate but equal" principle, and it would be the law of the land from the late 1800s until the late 1960s. Across the country were vivid reminders that blacks were second-class citizens. Signs that read "Whites Only" or "Colored" hung over water fountains and above doors to rest rooms, restaurants, and theaters. Employers and landlords found ways to restrict blacks from the best opportunities. Businesses refused to serve black customers. And fewer and fewer black voters cast their ballots at election time, discouraged by rules and regulations or threats and intimidation. Freedom—its promise so strong at the end of the Civil War—had proved elusive.

Separate but Equal? *Plessy v. Ferguson*

In 1890 Louisiana passed the Separate Car Activities statute, which stated that all railway companies had to provide separate cars for whites and for people of other races. Passengers who sat in the wrong compartment faced a twenty-five-dollar fine or twenty days in jail. In 1892 a thirty-year-old shoemaker named Homer Plessy took a seat in the white car of a New Orleans train. When he refused to leave, he was arrested. Plessy decided to take his case to court, stating that the Separate Car Activities statute violated the Fourteenth Amendment. Louisiana judge John H. Ferguson ruled against him, but Plessy took his case to the U.S. Supreme Court. All but one of the justices decided the law was constitutional. The opinion never uses the phrase *separate but equal,* but the ruling set in motion a new standard: segregation was legal as long as blacks were provided with facilities "equal" to those of whites. Following is an excerpt from the Supreme Court's majority opinion.

THE OBJECT OF THE [FOURTEENTH] AMENDMENT was undoubtedly to enforce the absolute equality of the two races before the law, but . . . it could not have been intended to abolish distinctions based upon color, or to enforce social, as distinguished from political, equality, or a commingling of the two races upon terms unsatisfactory to either. Laws permitting, and even requiring, their separation, in places where they are liable to be brought into contact, do not necessarily imply the inferiority of either race.

We consider the underlying fallacy of the plaintiff's [Plessy's] argument to consist in the assumption that the enforced separation of the two races stamps the colored race with a badge of inferiority. If this be so, it is not by reason of anything found in the act, but solely because the colored race chooses to put that construction upon it. . . . The argument also assumes that social prejudices may be overcome by legislation, and that equal rights cannot be secured to

affinities
positive feelings

the negro except by an enforced commingling of the two races. We cannot accept this proposition. If the two races are to meet upon terms of social equality, it must be the result of natural affinities. . . . Legislation is powerless to eradicate racial instincts, or to abolish distinctions based upon physical differences, and the attempt to do so can only result in accentuating the difficulties of the present situation. If the civil and political rights of both races be equal, one cannot be inferior to the other civilly . . . or politically. If one race be inferior to the other socially, the Constitution of the United States cannot put them upon the same plane.

> *"Legislation is powerless to eradicate racial instincts."*

—*From U.S. Supreme Court,* Plessy v. Ferguson, *163 U.S. 537 (1896), 163 U.S. 537.*

THINK ABOUT THIS

1. The Court decision said there is a difference between social equality and political equality. What does this mean? Can you have one form of equality without the other?
2. The justices said that laws cannot "eradicate racial instincts"—in other words, laws cannot end prejudice. Do you believe this is true?
3. Who would be in charge of deciding what was considered "equal"?

A Lone Voice for Equality: Justice Harlan Speaks Out

Only one justice, a Southerner named John Marshall Harlan, disagreed with the Plessy decision. Harlan said plainly that the Court had made separation of the races—and racial prejudice—an acceptable fact of American life. "The thin disguise of 'equal' accommodations . . . will not mislead anyone," wrote Harlan, "nor atone for the wrong done this day." Harlan's words proved to be true. From restaurants to schools, theaters to drinking fountains, segregation became a way of life. Following is a portion of Harlan's opinion.

Justice John Marshall Harlan, a Southerner, had once owned slaves, yet he is known today as the lone voice of opposition to the Plessy decision.

THE WHITE RACE deems itself to be the dominant race in this country. And so it is, in prestige, in achievements, in education, in wealth and in power. . . . But in view of the Constitution, in the eye of the law, there is in this country no superior, dominant, ruling class of citizens. There is no caste here. Our Constitution is color-blind, and neither knows nor tolerates classes among citizens. In respect of civil rights, all citizens are equal before the law. The humblest is the peer of the most powerful. The law regards man as man, and takes no account of his surroundings or of his color when his civil rights as guaranteed by the supreme law of the land are involved. . . .

"Our Constitution is color-blind."

The present decision . . . will not only stimulate aggressions . . . upon the admitted rights of colored citizens, but will encourage the belief that it is possible, by means of state enactments, to defeat the . . . purposes which the people of the United States had in view when they adopted the recent amendments of the Constitution. . . . Sixty millions of whites are in no danger from the presence here of eight millions of blacks. The destinies of the two races, in this country, are indissolubly linked together, and the interests of both require that the common government of all shall not permit the seeds of race hate to be planted under the sanction of law. What can more certainly arouse race hate, what more certainly create and perpetuate a feeling of distrust between these races, than state enactments, which, in fact, proceed on the ground that colored citizens are so inferior and degraded that they cannot be allowed to sit in public coaches occupied by white citizens? That, as all will admit, is the real meaning of such legislation as was enacted in Louisiana.

—From U.S. Supreme Court, Plessy v. Ferguson, *163 U.S. 537 (1896), 163 U.S. 537.*

THINK ABOUT THIS

1. According to Harlan, what effect would laws such as the Louisiana statute have?
2. What did Harlan believe was the real meaning of the Louisiana statute?

Song for a Sharecropper: Josh White Sings in Protest

So what was life like for African Americans after the Civil War amendments and *Plessy v. Ferguson*? Songwriter Josh White, born in 1915, used music to tell the story, and it was a story he knew too well.

At age seven he watched, unable to do a thing, as white deputies savagely beat his father for late payment of a bill. His father died from the beating. Young Josh, shoeless, scared, and hungry, left home to help support his family. In these difficult circumstances, he learned to play the guitar and to write his own music. As an adult White would help introduce the music of black Americans—black folk, blues, and spirituals—to the rest of the world. Josh White's songs were not usually about happy subjects; his simple lyrics were often deadly serious, questioning the American way of life. Speaking out against racism was dangerous for an African American, but White wrote, performed, and recorded songs of social protest. Following are his lyrics for "Southern Exposure," a song describing the life of a black farmworker in the South. Called sharecroppers, workers such as this man received poor pay or a small percentage of a crop in exchange for long, backbreaking hours in the fields. Many former slaves—and African Americans for generations to follow—worked as sharecroppers. This system was proof of how little life had changed for most Southern blacks after the Civil War.

A hand-painted photograph from 1902 depicts an Alabama sharecropper's family.

Well, I work all the week in the blazing sun,
Lord, I work all the week in the blazing sun,
Lord, I work all the week in the blazing sun,
Can't buy no shoes, Lord, when my payday comes.

I ain't treated no better than a mountain goat,
I ain't treated no better than a mountain goat,
I ain't treated no better, Lord, than a mountain goat,
Boss takes my crops and the poll tax takes my vote.

I'm leavin' here 'cause I just can't stay,
Yes, I'm leavin' here . . . I just can't stay,
Lord, I'm leavin', leavin' here 'cause I just can't stay,
I'm going where I can get more decent pay.

—"Southern Exposure," by Josh White, 1941.

poll tax
a tax levied by some states that required payment before a citizen could vote. The 24th Amendment to the Constitution outlawed the practice in 1964.

THINK ABOUT THIS

According to Josh White's lyrics, why was sharecropping an unfair way for people to earn a living?

A Visit to a Jim Crow School

No one was fooled by the "separate but equal" principle. Facilities for black people were never equal to those of their white counterparts, and in few places was this more apparent than in the public schools. In 1948 Ray Sprigle, a reporter for the *Pittsburgh Post-*

Gazette, posed as a black man and traveled to the South to understand what life was like for the ten million Americans living in the shadow of Jim Crow. The result was a twenty-one-part series called *I Was a Negro in the South for 30 Days.* The experience was extraordinary not only for Sprigle, but for his readers as well. "I quit being white, and free, and an American citizen when I climbed aboard that Jim Crow coach," wrote Sprigle. "From then on, until I came up out of the South four weeks later, I was black, and in bondage—not quite slavery but not quite freedom, either." Following is an excerpt from Sprigle's report on a segregated school in Georgia.

HERE ON THE OUTSKIRTS OF the pleasant, thriving little Georgia town of Bluffton in Clay county I go to school again. And what a school! This dilapidated, sagging old shack, leaning and lop-sided as its makeshift foundations give way, is the lordly white's conception of a schoolhouse for Negroes.

This leaking old wreck of a shanty must be nearly half a century old. The warped old clapboards are falling off. Holes bigger than your hand give permanent cross-ventilation. There are no desks, no seats but rude benches. Two rough tables serve as desks. . . .

Only redeeming feature of this thing called a school is the teacher. Tall and spare, gentle and soft spoken, earnest and intelligent, she reminds you of a typical New England school-marm with her sharp aquiline features—except for a deeper sun tan than one could ever get on a beach.

"The state furnishes us free school books now," she says. "When I started in 27 years ago the only text book we had was my Bible that I brought to school." . . .

OPEN JIM-CROW SCHOOL IN PENNSYLVANIA TOWN.

JOHNSTOWN, PA. — Arrangements have been made by the board of school directors, Rosedale borough, to conduct a special school in that district for the Colored children. During the past few months a large number of Colored families have moved to Rosedale from the south.

M. S. Bentz, county superintendent of schools, has secured two Colored instructors, Mr. Johnson and Miss Matthews, for the Rosedale school directors. Mr. Johnson is a graduate of Cornell university and has had much experience as a teacher. Miss Matthews is a graduate of a training school for teachers in South Carolina. She has specialized in work along industrial lines.

The Rosedale school opened Monday, Sept. 17. Approximately 110 Colored children were enrolled in the school.

This 1917 newspaper article announces the opening of a Jim Crow school in Pennsylvania.

There are 38 children in her school, divided into seven grades. She teaches them all. If all of her 38 scholars came to school at one time the little room would be crowded to suffocation. But now there is only a handful of little tots. All the bigger girls and boys are "excused." This is cotton chopping time and cotton is more important than learning. The bigger boys and girls are also "excused" at plowing and planting time and again in the fall when it's time to pick the precious cotton. The school term is eight months, she says. But only the little tots ever see eight months of schooling. . . .

[The] catchword . . . to justify . . . segregation with its inevitable train of discrimination, oppression, brutality and petty chicanery [deceit] is the term "separate but equal." . . . So far as the education of little black American citizens is concerned, that "equal" in the South's pet catch phrase is a brazen, cynical lie and every white man knows it.

No Negro school in all the South even begins to compare in any way with its companion white school . . . Right here in Clay county is a typical illustration of the bitter, tragic hypocrisy of that "separate but equal" lying catchword. Ride with me about a thousand yards down the highway past Minnie Dora Lee's disintegrating old rookery. On the edge of Bluffton is the school for the white folks. . . . A neat brick structure, with a wing on either side—at least six rooms.

Grounds beautifully landscaped, a spreading playground crowded with all the latest equipment that money can buy.

Minnie Dora Lee's school couldn't cost more than $1,000 even today. This white folks' school didn't cost a cent less than $100,000. "Separate but equal." It's not even funny.

—From Ray Sprigle, "A Visit to a Jim Crow School,"
Pittsburgh Post-Gazette, August 1948. To read more of the articles, visit:
http://www.postgazette.com/sprigle/default.asp

THINK ABOUT THIS

1. In what ways were black and white schools unequal?

2. Do you think it would have been permissible for white children to be "excused" from school in order to work?

The Right to a Fair Trial

Among the most significant rights of American citizens is the right to a fair trial. Apart from slavery, denial of that right is the most devastating injustice that black Americans have faced. Lynching is the execution, without a fair trial, of a person accused of a crime. Black men knew that they could become victims of lynching at any time, even if they were innocent of any wrongdoing. All it might take was the accusation of a white person. Victims were kidnapped by mobs and murdered—usually hanged or burned, often tortured as well. Records indicate that 3,386 African Americans—mostly men—were victims of lynching from 1882 to 1930, but the number of victims is almost certainly much higher, and the practice continued

Though difficult to comprehend, large crowds were known to gather and observe lynchings in a show of support. This picture was taken around 1933, during the Great Depression, when African Americans, in addition to being targets of racial bigotry, were also scapegoats for economic frustrations. The practice of lynching continued long after the Depression was over; no one is sure how many lives were lost in this way.

for many years. Following is a fictional account of a lynching. It is from *The Autobiography of an Ex-Coloured Man,* the story of a man whose light skin allows him to pass for white.

A SPACE WAS QUICKLY CLEARED in the crowd, and a rope placed about his neck, when from somewhere came the suggestion, "Burn him!" It ran like an electric current. Have you ever witnessed the transformation of human beings into savage beasts? Nothing can be more terrible. A railroad tie was sunk into the ground, the rope was removed, and a chain brought and securely coiled round the victim and the stake. There he stood, a man only in form and stature, every sign of degeneracy stamped upon his countenance. His eyes were dull and vacant, indicating not a single ray of thought. Evidently the realization of his fearful fate had robbed

"He was too stunned and stupefied even to tremble."

him of whatever reasoning power he had ever possessed. He was too stunned and stupefied even to tremble. Fuel was brought from everywhere, oil, the torch; the flames crouched for an instant as though to gather strength, then leaped up as high as their victim's head. He squirmed, he writhed, strained at his chains, then gave out cries and groans that I shall always hear. The cries and groans were choked off by the fire and smoke; but his eyes, bulging from the sockets, rolled from side to side, appealing in vain for help. Some of the crowd yelled and cheered, others seemed appalled at what they had done, and there were those who turned away sickened at the sight. I was fixed to the spot where I stood, powerless to take my eyes from what I did not want to see. . . . A great wave of humiliation and shame swept over me. Shame that I belonged to a race that could be so dealt with.

—*From James Weldon Johnson,* The Autobiography of an Ex-Coloured Man. *New York: Vintage Books, 1927. First published anonymously in 1912.*

THINK ABOUT THIS

1. Can you think of reasons white Southerners might have committed lynchings rather than allow the law to determine a black person's guilt or innocence?

2. Why did the narrator of this passage feel shame? How would you have felt in his place?

Many Americans—black and white alike—respected Booker T. Washington for his efforts to help African Americans. Over time, however, civil rights activists began to question whether his ideas would truly allow blacks to attain their full rights as citizens.

Chapter 2

Early Activists Take a Stand

AT THE DAWN OF THE TWENTIETH CENTURY, many African Americans accepted injustice and prejudice as a fact of life that couldn't be changed; to fight the status quo was to provoke trouble. Others, such as African-American educator Booker T. Washington, wanted to help blacks improve their lives, but not through protest. Instead, Washington felt blacks should tolerate discrimination, at least for a time. Meanwhile, he believed, they should obtain a practical schooling to gain skills that would help them find work, earn better wages, and improve their lives. Rather than focusing on an academic or intellectual education, Washington believed blacks should learn skills such as farming, mechanics, and housekeeping. With this in mind, he opened a school, the Tuskegee Institute, in Macon County, Alabama. The first of its kind, the institute encouraged students to learn work-based skills, setting aside civil rights activism and intellectual pursuits in favor of economic improvement. This, Washington promised, would lead to improved relations between the races, and civil rights would eventually follow.

Washington was considered the most influential black leader of his day, admired by both blacks and whites. But some African Americans did not agree with his strategy of acceptance and accommodation, especially at a time of increasing segregation and violence against blacks. They believed it was wrong to confine gifted and intelligent African Americans to menial, unsatisfying jobs simply because of their race. These activists, the earliest leaders of what would become the civil rights movement, believed the only way to end discrimination, racism, and prejudice was to fight these evils head-on, to take a stand for all American citizens, regardless of their color. In the readings that follow, you'll learn about early civil rights activists, courageous women and men who inspired future generations to wage war on racism.

Ida B. Wells: *A Red Record*

Among the most outspoken of early civil rights activists was the journalist Ida B. Wells. As the editor of the newspaper *Free Speech,* Wells wrote controversial articles about the injustices she witnessed in her town—Memphis, Tennessee. In 1892 she investigated the lynching of three black store owners who had been accused of assaulting a white woman. She concluded that the men had not committed the crime. They lost their lives, said Wells, because they were taking business away from the white owner of another store. When she published her findings, whites in the community were outraged. Her article called into question the most common excuse that Southerners gave for lynching—that black men were lynched as punishment for assaulting white women. In response to her article, angry whites destroyed the *Free Speech* office. Wells took refuge in the North, where she continued to write about anti-black violence and discrimination. In her 1895 pamphlet, *A Red Record,* she gave a brief history of lynching and then tallied the number that had occurred in 1893, providing some of the first statistics on the subject. She also offered sympathetic white readers suggestions of ways to stop lynching. Wells's work contributed to the anti-lynching movement, a cause that would soon be taken up by women of both races, North and South. Following is an excerpt from Wells's *A Red Record.*

Ida B. Wells enjoyed a successful career as a journalist and an activist—a remarkable achievement for a black woman of her day. In 1990 the U.S. Postal Service issued a stamp in her honor.

DURING THE SLAVE REGIME, the Southern white man owned the Negro body and soul. It was to his interest to dwarf the soul and preserve the body. Vested with unlimited power over his slave, to subject him to any and all kinds of physical punishment, the white man was still restrained from such punishment as tended to injure the slave by abating [decreasing] his physical powers and thereby reducing his financial worth. While slaves were scourged [whipped] mercilessly, and in countless cases inhumanly treated in other respects, still the white owner rarely permitted his anger to go so far as to take a life, which would entail upon him a loss of several hundred dollars. The slave was rarely killed, he was too valuable. . . .

But Emancipation came and the vested interests of the white man in the Negro's body were lost. The white man had no right to scourge the emancipated Negro, still less has he a right to kill him. . . . In slave times the Negro was kept subservient and submissive by the frequency and severity of the scourging, but, with freedom, a new system of intimidation came into vogue; the Negro was not only whipped and scourged; he was killed. . . .

> *". . . the Negro was not only whipped and scourged; he was killed."*

Not all nor nearly all of the murders done by white men, during the past thirty years [1865–1895] in the South have come to light, but the statistics as gathered and preserved by white men, and which have not been questioned, show that during these years more than ten thousand Negroes have been killed in cold blood, without the formality of judicial trial and legal execution. And yet . . . the same record shows that during all these years, and for all these murders [lynchings] only three white men have been tried, convicted, and executed.

—*From Ida B. Wells,* A Red Record, *1895. Reprinted in Jacqueline Jones Royster, editor,* Southern Horrors and Other Writings: The Anti-Lynching Campaign of Ida B. Wells, 1892–1900. *Boston: Bedford Books, 1997. Full text is available at http://womhist.binghamton.edu/aswpl/doc4.htm*

THINK ABOUT THIS

1. According to Wells, why were black people rarely punished with death when slavery was still legal?
2. Wells noted that few white men were ever punished for lynching. What explanation can you give for this?

W. E. B. Du Bois: On Booker T. Washington

A writer, an intellectual, and a social scientist, W. E. B. Du Bois is considered one of the most influential African Americans prior to the modern civil rights movement. Du Bois was the first African American to earn a doctorate from Harvard University. Once out of school, he began to conduct research on the lives of black Americans. But as he pursued this work, Du Bois realized he "could not be a calm, cool, and detached scientist while Negroes were lynched, murdered, and starved." Increasingly, he began to speak out as an activist and social critic. In 1903 he published a collection of essays, *The Souls of Black Folk,* which many call the most important book ever written by an African American. In it Du Bois said that the "color line" was the most serious problem the United States would face in the twentieth century. Following is a portion of an essay from that collection, "Of Mr. Booker T. Washington and Others."

MR. WASHINGTON DISTINCTLY ASKS that black people give up, at least for the present, three things,—

First, political power,

Second, insistence on civil rights,

Third, higher education of Negro youth,—and concentrate all their energies on industrial education, and accumulation of wealth, and the conciliation of the South. This policy has been courageously and insistently advocated for over fifteen years. . . . In these years there have occurred:

1. The disfranchisement of the Negro.
2. The legal creation of a distinct status of civil inferiority for the Negro.
3. The steady withdrawal of aid from institutions for the higher training of the Negro.

These movements are not, to be sure, direct results of Mr. Washington's teachings; but his propaganda has, without a shadow of doubt, helped their speedier accomplishment. . . .

It would be unjust to Mr. Washington not to acknowledge that in several instances he has opposed movements in the South which were

Students at Booker T. Washington's Tuskegee Institute learned skills that would help them succeed economically but took no academic courses. W. E. B. Du Bois did not agree with the school's philosophy. He believed blacks could not achieve equality without higher education and political activism.

unjust to the Negro; . . . he has spoken against lynching, and in other ways has openly or silently set his influence against sinister schemes and unfortunate happenings. Notwithstanding this, it is equally true to assert that on the whole the distinct impression left by Mr. Washington's propaganda is, first, that the South is justified in its present attitude toward the Negro because of the Negro's degradation; secondly, that the prime cause of the Negro's failure to rise more quickly is his wrong education in the past; and, thirdly, that his future rise depends primarily on his own efforts. Each of these propositions is a dangerous half-truth. . . . [F]irst, slavery and race-prejudice are potent if not sufficient causes of the Negro's position; second, industrial and common-school training were necessarily slow in planting because they had to await the black teachers trained by higher institutions . . . and, third, while it is a great truth to say that the Negro must strive and strive mightily to help himself, it is equally true that unless his striving be not simply seconded, but rather aroused and encouraged, by the initiative of the richer and wiser environing [surrounding] group, he cannot hope for great success.

". . . the hands of none of us are clean if we bend not our energies to righting these great wrongs."

In his failure to realize and impress this last point, Mr. Washington is especially to be criticised. His doctrine has tended to make the whites, North and South, shift the burden of the Negro problem to the Negro's shoulders and stand aside as critical and rather pessimistic spectators; when in fact the burden belongs to the nation, and the hands of none of us are clean if we bend not our energies to righting these great wrongs.

—From W. E. B. Du Bois, "Of Mr. Booker T. Washington and Others," in The Souls of Black Folk, *Cambridge, MA: A. C. McClurg & Co., 1903. Full text is available at* http://www.knowledgerush.com/books/soulb10html

1. Du Bois believed the increasing negative feelings between whites and blacks would be the biggest problem Americans would face in the twentieth century. According to this essay, how had Booker T. Washington contributed to this problem?
2. What did Du Bois claim had caused "the Negro's degradation"?
3. Washington believed that African Americans were responsible for their own lives and futures. What was Du Bois's viewpoint on this issue?

A Call for Justice: The NAACP

In 1908, horrified by a race riot in Springfield, Illinois, a group of black and white activists organized a meeting to discuss racism. Sixty people attended and later signed the Platform of the National Negro Committee. This committee would soon evolve into an organization called the National Association for the Advancement of Colored People, or NAACP. Only seven of the sixty people who signed the document were African American, but among those seven were prominent leaders, including Ida B. Wells, W. E. B. Du Bois, and educator and activist Mary Church Terrell. Within ten years, the NAACP would have more than 90,000 members, African-American leadership, and branches in three hundred U.S. cities. Opposing Booker T. Washington's approach of caution and patience, members of the NAACP were unwilling to wait for things to get better. They demanded change; through court battles, protests, and activism, they would work to ensure that black citizens be granted the same rights as whites and that the Civil War amendments be enforced. Following is the National Negro Committee platform (later adopted by the

NAACP), which was signed on February 12, 1909, the centennial of Abraham Lincoln's birth.

WE DENOUNCE THE EVER-GROWING OPPRESSION of our 10,000,000 colored fellow citizens as the greatest menace that threatens the country. Often plundered of their just share of the public funds, robbed of nearly all part in the government, segregated by common carriers, some murdered . . . , and all treated with open contempt by officials, they are held in some States in practical slavery to the white community. The systematic persecution of law-abiding citizens and their disfranchisement on account of their race alone is a crime that will ultimately drag down to an infamous end any nation that allows it to be practiced. . . .

When the NAACP was founded in 1909, much of its membership was white. As time passed, increasing numbers of African Americans joined the organization. This photograph, taken at the twenty-third annual conference in 1932, shows that by that time, the majority of the NAACP leadership was African American.

We agree fully with the prevailing opinion that the transformation of the unskilled colored laborers in industry and agriculture into skilled workers is of vital importance to that race and to the nation, but we demand for the Negroes, as for all others, a free and complete education, whether by city, State or nation, a grammar school and industrial training for all and technical, professional, and academic education for the most gifted.

"...the Negro... will never receive a fair and equal treatment until he is given equal treatment in the Legislature."

But . . . the Negro . . . will never receive a fair and equal treatment until he is given equal treatment in the Legislature and before the law. Nor will the practically educated Negro, no matter how valuable to the community he may prove, be given a fair return for his labor or encouraged to put forth his best efforts or given the chance to develop that efficiency that comes only outside the school until he is respected in his legal rights as . . . a citizen. . . .

As first and immediate steps toward remedying these national wrongs, . . . we demand of Congress and the Executive:

(1) That the Constitution be strictly enforced and the civil rights guaranteed under the Fourteenth Amendment be secured impartially to all.

(2) That there be equal educational opportunities for all and in all the States, and that public school expenditure be the same for the Negro and white child.

(3) That in accordance with the Fifteenth Amendment the right of the Negro to the ballot on the same terms as other citizens be recognized in every part of the country.

—*Platform Adopted by the National Negro Committee, 1909. Available at the Library of Congress Web site: http://memory.loc.gov/ammem/aaohtml/exhibit/aopart6b.html*

1. What was meant by the term *practical slavery*?
2. How did the platform address the philosophy of Booker T. Washington? To what extent did it support Washington's ideas? To what extent did it differ from the educator's views?

A Heated Debate at the White House

William Monroe Trotter was a Harvard-educated activist and the editor of a Boston newspaper for African Americans, *The Guardian.* Trotter had supported Democratic candidate Woodrow Wilson in the election of 1912, but the new president's actions would sorely disappoint him. President Wilson created segregation policies for the U.S. government, such as rules barring black and white postal clerks from working together. In 1914 Trotter wrote a letter requesting a meeting with the president, and Wilson agreed. Trotter arrived at the White House with a small delegation of black activists. The two men argued heatedly for forty-five minutes before Trotter and his companions were escorted out of the White House. Trotter was banned from returning for the rest of Wilson's term. When Trotter left the building, he spoke to reporters about what had happened. The excerpt below is taken from a front-page article of the *New York Times* that appeared the following day.

WASHINGTON, NOV. 12—Segregation of white and negro civil service employees in Government departments, a system inaugurated during the present Administration, is to be continued. President Wilson

made clear his views on the subject today when he received a delegation representing the National Independence Equal Rights League.
The President resented the attitude of the spokesman, William Monroe Trotter, of Boston, who was quoted as having attempted to cross-
examine Mr. Wilson, when the President explained that the question
was not a political one, and that he
would not be influenced in his decision
by the threats of the league to oppose
the Democratic Party.

President Wilson informed the delegation that never since he had been in
office had he been addressed in such an
insulting fashion. He said that if at any
time in the future he should consent to
receive representatives of the league,
that body would have to designate
another spokesman. . . .

The President said the policy of segregation had been enforced for the
comfort and best interests of both races
in order to overcome friction. He made
it clear that he had endeavored in every
way to assist the negro race toward its
independent development. . . .

William Monroe Trotter was an outspoken critic
of the status quo. Offended by Trotter's "tone,
with its background of passion," Woodrow
Wilson banned Trotter from the White House
for the rest of his presidential term.

When the President had concluded
his remarks, Trotter stepped forward
and began questioning Mr. Wilson. He
suggested that unless the Administration abandoned the segregation
policy the Democratic Party could expect the united opposition of the
negro voters in 1916. . . .

The mention of votes caused Mr. Wilson to say that politics must
be left out, because it was a form of blackmail. . . . Mr. Wilson urged
that he wanted his auditors to understand that it was a human problem and not a political problem. . . .

Once outside Trotter said:

"What the President told us was entirely disappointing. His statement that segregation was intended to prevent racial friction is not supported by facts. For fifty years negro and white employees have worked together in the Government departments in Washington. It was not until the present Administration came in that segregation was drastically introduced."

"What the President told us was entirely disappointing."

—From *"President Resents Negro's Criticism,"* New York Times, *November 13, 1914.*

THINK ABOUT THIS

1. What did Wilson cite as his reason for creating the segregation policy? What did Trotter think of this explanation?

2. Wilson said he resented Trotter's attitude. How do you think Trotter behaved at the meeting? If he was rude to the president, do you think he had a right to be? If he had been polite, would Wilson have reacted any differently to Trotter?

3. Do you agree with Wilson that segregation was "a human problem and not a political problem"?

A Poet's Defiant Appeal

In the first decades of the twentieth century, working-class whites increasingly resented having to compete with blacks for jobs. The summer of 1919 brought this resentment to a peak, as race riots broke out around the country, from Texas to Chicago to Washington, D.C. It was during Red Summer, as this period of violence became known, that African-American poet Claude McKay, then working on a railroad dining car, wrote one of his most famous poems, "If We Must Die." This defiant poem told black Americans to rebel against anti-black violence. It also heralded what many consider to be the beginning of the Harlem Renaissance, a period of great artistic and cultural achievement among African-American writers, musicians, and artists. Here is McKay's explanation of what led him to write "If We Must Die," followed by the poem.

"THE WORLD WAR [WORLD WAR I] had ended. But its end was a signal for the outbreak of little wars between labor and capital and, like a plague breaking out in sore places, between colored folk and white. Our Negro newspapers were morbid, full of details of clashes between colored and white, murderous shootings and hangings.

Traveling from city to city and unable to gauge the attitude and temper of each one, we Negro railroad men were nervous. We were less light-hearted. We did not separate from one another gaily to spend ourselves in speakeasies and gambling joints. We stuck together, some of us armed, going from the railroad station to our quarters. We stayed in our quarters all through the dreary ominous nights, for we never knew what was going to happen. . . . It was during those days that the sonnet, "If We Must Die," exploded out of me.

Claude McKay published his first book of poetry at the age of twenty. Both his work and his ideals inspired younger poets, including Langston Hughes, to follow in his footsteps.

IF WE MUST DIE

If we must die—let it not be like hogs
Hunted and penned in an inglorious spot,
While round us bark the mad and hungry dogs,
Making their mock at our accursed lot.
If we must die—oh, let us nobly die,
So that our precious blood may not be shed
In vain; then even the monsters we defy
Shall be constrained to honor us though dead!

Oh, Kinsmen! We must meet the common foe;
Though far outnumbered, let us show us brave,
And for their thousand blows deal one deathblow!
What though before us lies the open grave?
Like men we'll face the murderous, cowardly pack,
Pressed to the wall, dying, but fighting back!

—From Claude McKay, A Long Way from Home. *New York:
Arno-New York Times, 1969. Original work published in 1937.*

THINK ABOUT THIS

1. What is the "outbreak of little wars" to which McKay referred? Who was fighting these wars?

2. What symbolism did McKay use to describe violent white rioters in the poem?

Chapter 3

Breaking Barriers: The Road to Change

WITH EACH NEW DECADE of the twentieth century, more African Americans were frustrated and angered by the discrimination that challenged nearly every aspect of their lives. And more African Americans were ready to take a stand. Fighting injustice took courage and involved great risk, but it had become too difficult to passively accept things as they were.

After two World Wars, black soldiers wanted an end to segregation in the military. The acclaimed civil rights lawyer Charles Hamilton Houston served in the segregated army during World War I. It was his experience in the military that convinced him to become a lawyer. "The hate and scorn showered on us Negro officers by our fellow Americans," said Houston, "convinced me that there was no sense in my dying for a world ruled by them. I made up my mind that if I got through this war I would study law and use my time fighting for men who could not strike back." During World War II, African-American soldiers struggled with the fact

Civil rights activists confronted discrimination in every aspect of American life. Among the most celebrated challenges to segregation took place in 1947, when Jackie Robinson broke baseball's color line and integrated the major league.

that their nation fought injustice overseas but allowed discrimination at home. Poet Langston Hughes brought the contradiction to America's attention in his 1943 poem "Beaumont to Detroit" in which a black soldier asks,

Yet you say we're fightin
For democracy.
Then why don't democracy
include me?
I ask you this question
Cause I want to know
How long I got to fight
BOTH HITLER—AND JIM CROW?

Likewise, African Americans wanted equal opportunities in education and employment—not only in the Jim Crow South, but in the North as well. They wanted the right to live in any neighborhood, to eat in any restaurant, to attend any concert or event and take any seat they chose.

Activists found different ways to fight the system. Some bravely defied segregation laws, refusing to tolerate humiliating policies. Others took action through the courts. Regardless of the method, their courage would lead the way to change. The following selections tell the stories of the Americans who first crossed the color line—in places as diverse as the stage and the armed forces, public buses and the ballpark.

Charles Hamilton Houston and the Law

An exceptional student, Charles Hamilton Houston graduated from Harvard University in the top 5 percent of his class. Houston saw the law as the key to fighting Jim Crow. He became a professor at Howard University, where he trained future black lawyers to join the legal assault on segregation. As Houston became more well known, the NAACP began to request his help. Its members were determined to overturn *Plessy v. Ferguson.* By the early 1930s Houston was the organization's chief legal counsel. He decided that the place to begin revoking the separate but equal doctrine was public education. In 1935 a young man named Lloyd Gaines, an excellent student and president of his college class, was denied admission to the law school at the University of Missouri. Three years later Houston and the NAACP took his case to the Supreme Court. Following is the Court's decision in the case—the first in a series of victories that would eventually topple the separate but equal principle, forcing states to provide educational opportunities that were truly equal for all.

IT WAS ADMITTED ON THE TRIAL that petitioner's "work and credits at the Lincoln University would qualify him for admission to the School of Law of the University of Missouri if he were found otherwise eligible." He was refused admission upon the ground that it was "contrary to the constitution, laws and public policy of the State to admit a negro as a student in the University of Missouri." It appears that there are schools of law in connection with the state universities of four adjacent States, Kansas, Nebraska, Iowa and Illinois, where nonresident negroes are admitted. . . .

Charles Houston (*right*) worked with an up-and-coming NAACP lawyer named Thurgood Marshall (*standing*) on the *Gaines* case. They are shown here with Gaines in a photograph taken during the trial.

The basic consideration is . . . what opportunities Missouri itself furnishes to white students and denies to negroes solely upon the ground of color. . . . By the operation of the laws of Missouri a privilege has been created for white law students which is denied to negroes by reason of their race. The white resident is afforded legal education within the State; the negro resident having the same qualifications is refused it there and must go outside the State to obtain it. That is a denial of the equality of legal right to the enjoyment of the privilege which the State has set up, and the provision for the payment of tuition fees in another State does not remove the discrimination. . . .

We are of the opinion that . . . [the] petitioner was entitled to be admitted to the law school of the State University in the absence of other and proper provision for his legal training within the State.

—*From* Missouri ex rel. Gaines v. Canada, Registrar of the University of Missouri, et al. *No. 57, Supreme Court of the United States, 305 U.S. 337 (1938).*

1. Although the Supreme Court decided in Gaines's favor, it did not go so far as to strike down the separate but equal doctrine established by *Plessy v. Ferguson*. What words in the decision tell us this?

2. How did the state of Missouri bypass federal laws that required it to offer the same educational opportunities to blacks that whites enjoyed?

Segregation in the Capital: Marian Anderson Sings for Freedom

On Easter Sunday 1939, a crowd gathered at the Lincoln Memorial to hear the world-famous singer Marian Anderson perform. The event was to have taken place at Constitution Hall, but the Daughters of the American Revolution (DAR), the organization that ran the hall, refused to let a black singer perform there. First Lady Eleanor Roosevelt was a member of the DAR; she was also a dedicated opponent of discrimination. Roosevelt demanded that the DAR reconsider its decision; when the organization refused, she publicly gave up her membership, and the DAR's policy of discrimination became a national controversy. Roosevelt and other activists arranged for Anderson to perform at the Lincoln Memorial. More than 75,000 people arrived to hear her—the largest crowd that had ever assembled there. Millions more listened to the concert on the radio. Although the incident had been a painful one for Anderson, her performance was a symbol of achievement for those who struggled for civil rights. Following is an account of the concert as told by Walter White, the general secretary of the NAACP.

NO MEMBER OF THAT AUDIENCE will ever forget the sight of Miss Anderson emerging from a small anteroom beside Gauden's statue of Lincoln. She was apparently calm, but those of us who knew her were aware of the great perturbation beneath her serene exterior. . . . A tremendous wave of applause rose from the vast throng, which was silenced only when Miss Anderson gently raised her hand to ask that the concert be permitted to begin. Amplifiers poured out the thunderous chords of the opening bars of "America." Clasping her hands before her Miss Anderson poured out in her superb voice "sweet land of liberty" almost as though it was a prayer.

As the last notes of "Nobody Knows the Trouble I've Seen" faded

Marian Anderson at the Lincoln Memorial, April 9, 1939. "Sometimes you're overwhelmed when a thing comes, and you do not realize the magnitude of the affair at that moment," Anderson said. "When you get away from it, you wonder, did it really happen to you?"

away the spell was broken by the rush of the audience toward Miss Anderson. . . . [A] single figure caught my eye in the mass of people below which seemed one of the most important and touching symbols of the occasion. It was a slender black girl dressed in somewhat too garishly hued Easter finery. Hers was not the face of one who had been the beneficiary of much education or opportunity. Her hands were particularly noticeable as she thrust them forward and upward, trying desperately, although she was some distance away from Miss Anderson, to touch the singer. They were hands which despite their youth had known only the dreary work of manual labor. Tears streamed down the girl's dark face. Her hat was askew, but in her eyes flamed hope bordering on ecstasy. Life which had been none too easy for her now held out greater hope because one who was also colored and who, like herself, had known poverty, privation, and prejudice, had, by her genius, gone a long way toward conquering bigotry. If Marian Anderson could do it, the girl's eyes seemed to say, then I can, too.

"Miss Anderson poured out . . . 'sweet land of liberty' almost as though it was a prayer."

—*From Walter White,* A Man Called White: The Autobiography of Walter White. *New York: Viking Press, 1948.*

THINK ABOUT THIS

1. Among her selections, Miss Anderson chose to sing "America" ("My Country 'Tis of Thee") and the spiritual "Nobody Knows the Trouble I've Seen." Why do you think she chose these songs?

2. Why was Anderson's appearance at the Lincoln Memorial such an important event?

Taking It to Court: Thurgood Marshall and the Legal Process

In 1933 Charles Houston asked one of his former students to work for him at the NAACP. "The Association needs another full-time lawyer in the national office," he wrote. "I don't know of anybody I would rather have in the national office than you." The young man's name was Thurgood Marshall, and he accepted Houston's offer. Five years later, after Houston's resignation, Marshall became the organization's new chief counsel; down the road, he would become the first African-American Supreme Court justice. Like Houston, Marshall firmly believed that it was through the law that people could most effectively fight discrimination. With Marshall at the helm, the NAACP won many cases, and it was Marshall who would eventually bring an end to legal segregation. Following is an excerpt from a 1942 speech in which he explained how individuals could bring a case to court with the help of the NAACP.

THERE IS NO REASON WHY a hundred clear cases . . . should not be placed before the United States Attorneys and the Attorney General every year until the election officials discover that it is both wiser and safer to follow the United States laws than to violate them. It is up to us to see that these officials of the Department of Justice are called upon to act again and again wherever there are violations of the civil rights statutes. Unfortunately, there are plenty of such cases. It is equally unfortunate that there are not enough individuals and groups presenting these cases and demanding action. . . .

The NAACP can move no faster than the individuals who have been discriminated against. We only take up cases where we are requested to do so by persons who have been discriminated against. . . .

. . . [I]t seems clear that although it is necessary and vital to all of us that we continue our program for additional legislation to guarantee and enforce certain of our rights, at the same time we must continue with ever-increasing vigor to enforce those few statutes, both federal and state, which are now on the statute books. We must not be delayed by people who say "the time is not ripe". . . . Persons who deny to us our civil rights should be brought to justice now. Many people believe the time is always "ripe" to discriminate against Negroes. All right then—the time is always "ripe" to bring them to justice. The responsibility for the enforcement of these statutes rests with every American citizen regardless of race or color. However, the real job has to be done by the Negro population with whatever friends of the other races are willing to join us.

> *"Persons who deny to us our civil rights should be brought to justice now."*

—From Thurgood Marshall, "The Legal Attack to Secure Civil Rights," July 13, 1942.
Speech given at the NAACP Wartime Conference, Chicago, IL.

THINK ABOUT THIS

1. Did Marshall want to create new laws to fight discrimination?
2. According to Marshall, why weren't many civil rights cases being presented to the courts?

A Television Report: Excellent News at Hand

On July 26, 1948, President Harry Truman issued an executive order to end segregation in the army. The U.S. Air Force immediately complied with Truman's order and recruited more African Americans, assigning them to units on the basis of merit alone. No more would talented black soldiers be assigned to all-black units, nor would they be relegated to the least challenging or exciting posts. The army and navy resisted integration, but it would come to their ranks with or without their cooperation. At the start of the Korean War in 1950, thousands of black men, inspired by Truman's executive order, enlisted in the armed forces—too many to fit into existing all-black units. Integration happened naturally, and without the problems that many had anticipated. By 1953, 95 percent of African-American soldiers were serving in integrated units. Following is a television news report from February 27, 1950, reporting on the state of segregation in the armed forces.

THERE IS SOME EXCELLENT NEWS at hand right now about the normally bad situation of racial discrimination in the Armed Forces. Months ago the President appointed the Fahy Committee to push for equality in the services, and the reports from field surveys are coming in. The Army is just beginning to integrate Negroes and whites in its jobs and schools. But Air Force and Navy have already made some real progress. There are 26,000 Negroes in the Air Force; 71 per cent are now completely integrated—sleeping, studying, working, eating side by side with whites. In a few months, all will be integrated. Field investigators now find the Officer and Service Clubs without discrimination. They find Negroes and whites together at the Air Force swim-

During the Korean War integrated units saw combat for the first time in U.S. history. In many cases, long-held prejudices evaporated as white and black soldiers confronted the pressures of battle.

ming pools and dances. The amount of mixing varies from place to place. But it is none the less a remarkable change. And in every place the transition has occurred with remarkably little trouble. Even southern officers who personally do not like it tell the investigators, almost invariably, that the integration is working. There is less friction and not more. At the end of the war [World War II] 95 per cent of the Negroes . . . in the Navy were confined to the Steward branch [working as servants, cooks, or similar support staff]; today only 58

"... what is going on is a kind of quiet social revolution."

per cent. One can only suggest in this limited space the full story of what is happening. But as one of the field investigators puts it, what is going on is a kind of quiet social revolution. We feel, he said, that in time this will have an incalculable effect upon the civilian population.

—*From the* President's Secretary Files, Harry S. Truman Papers, *Harry S. Truman Library, Independence, MO.*

THINK ABOUT THIS

1. The reporter noted that fewer black soldiers were working in the Steward branch, that is, fewer were working as servants, cooks, or in other less prestigious posts. What significance does this have?

2. According to one field investigator, what effect would desegregation in the military have on the United States?

Jackie Robinson Plays Ball

Baseball is called the national pastime, but for the first half of the twentieth century the major league teams were just another aspect of American life that was closed to blacks. Then, in 1947, the Brooklyn Dodgers gave Jack Roosevelt Robinson the chance to be the first black to play major league baseball since the late 1800s, when the league banned African Americans from its ranks. Robinson had played for the Negro League's Kansas City Monarchs, but players for the Negro League teams received inferior pay and—no matter how outstanding—little recognition for their skill. As Robinson prepared for the Majors, the Dodgers' president, Branch Rickey,

Dodgers' president Branch Rickey offers a few words of wisdom as Jackie Robinson prepares to sign his contract. Rickey once said a great ballplayer was one who was brave enough to take a chance. Without question, Rickey had found that quality in Robinson.

warned him that he'd face a great challenge. Robinson would have to be willing to live with ridicule, hostility—perhaps even death threats. "I'm looking for a ballplayer with guts enough not to fight back," said Rickey. It would be far from easy, but Robinson was prepared. An excellent athlete, he had lettered in four sports at the University of California. He'd reached the rank of second lieutenant in the army. And like most black men of the day, he'd experienced plenty of discrimination. In fact, he'd been court-martialed—and found innocent—for refusing to sit in the back of a segregated army bus. His first days in the Majors were rocky, but Robinson went on to become the National League Rookie of the Year. In 1949 he was named the league's most valuable player; and with Jackie on the team, the Dodgers won six league championships. Following is his recollection of a game played against the Philadelphia Phillies early in his first season.

STARTING TO THE PLATE in the first inning, I could scarcely believe my ears. Almost as if it had been synchronized by some master conductor, hate poured forth from the Phillies dugout.

"Hey nigger why don't you go back to the cotton field where you belong?"

"They're waiting for you in the jungles, black boy!" . . .

"We don't want you here, nigger."

"Go back to the bushes!"

Those insults and taunts were only samples of the torrent of abuse which poured out from the Phillies dugout that April day.

I have to admit that this day, of all the unpleasant days in my life, brought me nearer to cracking up than I ever had been. Perhaps I should have become inured [hardened] to this kind of garbage, but I was in New York City and unprepared for the kind of barbarism from a northern team that I had come to associate with the Deep South. The abuse coming out of the Phillies dugout was being directed by the team's manager, Ben Chapman, a Southerner. I felt tortured and I tried just to

"What was I doing here turning the other cheek?"

play ball and ignore the insults. But it was really getting to me. What did the Phillies want from me? What, indeed, did Mr. Rickey expect of me? I was, after all, a human being. What was I doing here turning the other cheek as though I weren't a man? . . .

For one wild and rage-crazed minute I thought, "To hell with Mr. Rickey's 'noble experiment.' It's clear it won't succeed. . . ."

Then I thought of Mr. Rickey—how his family and friends had begged him not to fight for me and my people. I thought of all of his predictions, which had come true. Mr. Rickey had come to a cross-roads and made a lonely decision. I was at a crossroads. I would make mine. I would stay.

—From Jackie Robinson and Alfred Duckett, I Never Had It Made: An Autobiography. *Hopewell, NJ: The Ecco Press, 1995. Originally published by G. P. Putnam's Sons, 1972.*

THINK ABOUT THIS

1. Why do you think Branch Rickey chose Robinson to conduct this "noble experiment"?
2. Why did Robinson decide to stay on the team?

The arrest of Rosa Parks, captured in a sculpture that made its way to the National Portrait Gallery in Washington, D.C. Rosa Parks's quiet act of defiance made her an icon of the civil rights movement.

The Modern Movement Begins

N THE 1940S AND 1950S, the NAACP became increasingly powerful. With additional funds and bright young lawyers, the organization was prepared to take on important discrimination cases. Thurgood Marshall founded its Legal Defense and Educational Fund to bring such cases to trial—with great success. In case after case, NAACP lawyers chipped away at legal segregation, setting in motion the most revolutionary years of the civil rights movement.

In 1954 the Supreme Court gave a groundbreaking decision in *Brown v. Board of Education.* In this case, brought before the Court by Marshall, the Court decided that "separate but equal" was unconstitutional in U.S. public schools. Activists and lawyers soon began to apply the decision to segregation in other areas of public life as well. In effect, the Court had overturned the 1896 *Plessy v. Ferguson* decision.

Aside from African Americans, however, few people supported the *Brown* decision. Although the NAACP continued to work for the admission of black children to all-white schools, the South's policy of "massive resistance" to integration made *Brown* virtually meaningless. Southerners created laws to stop the NAACP from operating in their states. Organizations were formed to threaten and undermine civil rights activists at every turn. Worst of all, with increasing legal protection for blacks, racist whites turned more and more to violence to maintain the status quo.

Only one year after *Brown,* the Supreme Court made a second ruling, *Brown II,* regarding the enforcement of its historic decision. Concerned that rapid integration would lead to violence, *Brown II* said that the new policy could be enforced gradually, addressing the problems and concerns of specific communities. Many Southern whites viewed the decision as permission to fight integration. In towns and cities across the South, whites responded with calls for massive resistance—organized opposition in the form of intimidation, threats, violence, and riots—to any attempt to dismantle Jim Crow.

A Milestone in the Movement: Brown v. Board of Education

Before *Brown,* the NAACP had not directly challenged segregation. It had not attempted to desegregate schools and other places but had only tried to ensure that blacks had equal facilities. *Brown* accomplished something else. It attacked the principle of "separate but equal." The most important part of the case related to the elementary schools of Topeka, Kansas, where the schools for whites and blacks were essentially of equal quality. Therefore, the Topeka school system did not defy the *Plessy v. Ferguson* decision. In *Brown,* Marshall and his colleagues argued that restricted facilities, whether equal or not, violated the Fourteenth Amendment and denied children their civil rights. Following is the Court's opinion on the case.

TODAY, EDUCATION IS PERHAPS the most important function of state and local governments. . . . Today it is a principal instrument in awakening the child to cultural values, in preparing him for later professional training, and in helping him to adjust normally to his environment. In these days, it is doubtful that any child may reasonably be expected to succeed in life if he is denied the opportunity of an education. Such an opportunity, where the state has undertaken to provide it, is a right which must be made available to all on equal terms.

We come then to the question presented: Does segregation of children in public schools solely on the basis of race, even though the physical facilities and other . . . factors may be equal, deprive the children of the minority group of equal educational opportunities? We believe that it does.

. . . To separate them from others of similar age and qualifications

NAACP lawyers (*left to right*) George E. C. Hayes, Thurgood Marshall, and James M. Nabrit congratulate one another following the 1954 Supreme Court decision that effectively overturned the "separate but equal" principle.

solely because of their race generates a feeling of inferiority as to their status in the community that may affect their hearts and minds in a way unlikely ever to be undone. . . .

We conclude that in the field of public education the doctrine of "separate but equal" has no place. Separate educational facilities are inherently [by their nature] unequal. Therefore, we hold that the plaintiffs and others similarly situated for whom the actions have been brought are, by reason of the segregation complained of, deprived of the equal protection of the laws guaranteed by the Fourteenth Amendment.

"Separate educational facilities are inherently unequal."

—Brown et al. v. Board of Education of Topeka et al. *Supreme Court of the United States, 347 U.S. 483. December 9, 1952, Argued. May 17, 1954, Decided.*

THINK ABOUT THIS

1. Why, according to *Brown*, was the doctrine of "separate but equal" wrong?

2. What laws, according to the Court, did the *Plessy* decision violate?

A Poet Remembers: The Death of Emmett Till

About one year after the Supreme Court's decision to end segregation, a fourteen-year-old boy named Emmett Till was murdered in Money, Mississippi. Emmett was from Chicago; he was in Money visiting relatives. Before he left, his mother warned him that things were different in the South. "Be careful," she said. "If you have to get down on your knees and bow when a white person goes past, do it willingly." Emmett didn't understand the South's racist way of life. On August 28, 1955, he was brutally beaten and then shot, his body thrown into the Tallahatchie River, all apparently for talking to and perhaps whistling at a white woman named Carolyn Bryant. Bryant's husband and his half brother admitted to abducting Emmett from his uncle's house. They were tried one month later. An all-white jury found them innocent, claiming that the body was so mutilated, it could not absolutely be identified as Till. The murder provoked outrage around the nation. Blacks in the North recognized that such vio-

Emmett Louis Till in an undated portrait

lent racism could touch their lives. No one, North or South, would easily forget the murder of Emmett Till. Following are four stanzas from a poem by the celebrated African-American poet Gwendolyn Brooks. She wrote the poem from the point of view of Carolyn Bryant remembering the murder in terms of a fairy tale.

Poet Gwendolyn Brooks, photographed on the back steps of her home in the Bronzeville district, part of Chicago's South Side. Most of Bronzeville's residents were African Americans, and Emmett Till's family lived there as well. Perhaps living in Till's hometown inspired Brooks to compose her complex and thought-provoking poem about his murder.

. . . But there was something about the matter of the
    Dark Villain.
He should have been older, perhaps.
The hacking down of a villain was
    more fun to think about
When his menace possessed
    undisputed breadth, undisputed
    height,
And a harsh kind of vice.
And best of all, when his history was cluttered
With the bones of many eaten knights and princesses.

"He should have been older, perhaps."

The fun was disturbed, then all but nullified
When the Dark Villain was a blackish child
Of fourteen, with eyes still too young to be dirty,
And a mouth too young to have lost every reminder
Of its infant softness.

That boy must have been surprised! For
These were grown-ups. Grown-ups were supposed
    to be wise.
And the Fine Prince—and that other—so tall,
    so broad, so
Grown! Perhaps the boy had never guessed
That the trouble with grown-ups was that under the
    magnificent shell of adulthood, just under,
Waited the baby full of tantrums.

It occurred to her that there may have been something
Ridiculous in the picture of the Fine Prince
Rushing (rich with breadth and height and

Mature solidness whose lack, in the Dark Villain, was
    impressing her,
Confronting her more and more as this first day after the
    trial
And acquittal wore on) rushing
With his heavy companion to hack down (unhorsed)
That little foe.
So much had happened, she could not remember now
    what that foe had done
Against her, or if anything had been done.

*—From Gwendolyn Brooks, "A Bronzeville Mother Loiters in Mississippi.
Meanwhile, a Mississippi Mother Burns Bacon." Originally published
in* The Bean Eaters, *New York: Harpers, 1960. Available online
at http://www.reed.edu/%7Epaulsona/bronzeville.html*

THINK ABOUT THIS

1. The poem talks about the "Dark Villain" and the "Fine Prince." Who do these images represent?
2. Does the woman in the poem believe the Dark Villain deserved what happened to him?
3. Which of the villain's characteristics make the woman uncomfortable with what happened? Why does the poet describe the villain as "unhorsed"?

Rosa Parks Takes a Stand

Civil rights activist Rosa Parks joined the NAACP in 1943. She worked as a youth adviser, helped organize voter registration drives, and was elected secretary of the Montgomery, Alabama, chapter of the NAACP. Her involvement became personal on December 1, 1955. She was returning home by bus from her job as a seamstress. When the driver asked her to give up her seat to a white passenger, she refused. The front rows on Montgomery's buses were reserved for whites only. The law required blacks to give up their seats in the middle section when all the front seats were taken. Parks believed this law was unfair, and on that day in December 1955, she decided to fight it. The driver called the police, and Parks was arrested. Following is her recollection of the incident, which led to the first major protest of the modern civil rights movement.

HAVING TO TAKE A CERTAIN SECTION because of your race was humiliating, but having to stand up because a particular driver wanted to keep a white person from having to stand was, to my mind, most inhumane. . . .

December 1, 1955, I had finished my day's work as a tailor's assistant in the Montgomery Fair department store and I was on my way home. There was one vacant seat on the Cleveland Avenue bus, which I took, alongside a man and two women across the aisle. There were still a few vacant seats in the white section in the front, of course. We went to the next stop without being disturbed. On the third [stop], the front seats were occupied and this one man, a white man, was standing. The driver asked us to stand up and let him have those seats, and when none of us moved at his first words, he said, "You all make it light on yourselves and let me have those seats." And the man who was sitting next to the window stood up, and I made room for him to pass by me. The two women across the aisle stood up and moved out.

When the driver saw me still sitting, he asked if I was going to stand up, and I said, "No, I'm not."

And he said, "Well, if you don't stand up, I'm going to call the police and have you arrested."

I said, "You may do that."

He did get off the bus, and I still stayed where I was. Two policemen came on the bus. One of the policemen asked me if the bus driver had asked me to stand and I said yes.

He said, "Why don't you stand up?"

And I asked him, "Why do you push us around?"

"Why do you push us around?"

—*From Henry Hampton and Steve Fayer,* Voices of Freedom.
New York: Bantam Books, 1990.

Rosa Parks and a white passenger take a ride in Montgomery shortly after the Supreme Court found segregation on the city's buses to be unconstitutional.

A Boycott Turns the Tide

Civil rights activists in Montgomery went to work immediately after Parks was arrested. The Women's Political Council distributed more than 50,000 fliers announcing a boycott of the city buses, which was to take place on the day of Parks's trial. The one-day boycott turned into a 381-day protest, led by the Montgomery Improvement Association (MIA) and two young ministers, Martin Luther King Jr. and Ralph Abernathy. King, the head of the MIA, encouraged protesters to remain peaceful and dignified, never to resort to violence. The protesters' calm behavior contrasted sharply with threats from whites who opposed the boycott. Montgomery's buses moved virtually empty about the city as the black community walked, carpooled, bicycled, or took taxis. Meanwhile, the MIA took the bus system to court, and a district judge ordered the buses desegregated. The city refused to comply and took its case to the U.S. Supreme Court, which agreed with the judge's decision: Montgomery's buses must be integrated. The courage of one woman, and the determination of the city's black community, had made a tremendous difference. Here is the text of a flyer circulated at the boycott's end.

December 19, 1956

INTEGRATED BUS SUGGESTIONS
This is a historic week because segregation on buses has now been declared unconstitutional. Within a few days the Supreme Court Mandate will reach Montgomery and you will be re-boarding

integrated buses. This places upon us all a tremendous responsibility of maintaining, in the face of what could be some unpleasantness, a calm and loving dignity befitting good citizens and members of our Race. If there is violence in word or deed it must not be our people who commit it.

For your help and convenience the following suggestions are made. Will you read, study and memorize them so that our non-violent determination may not be endangered. First, some general suggestions:

"Not all white people are opposed to integrated buses."

1. Not all white people are opposed to integrated buses. Accept goodwill on the part of many.
2. The whole bus is now for the use of all people. Take a vacant seat.
3. Pray for guidance and commit yourself to complete non-violence in word and action as you enter the bus.
4. Demonstrate the calm dignity of our Montgomery people in your actions.
5. In all things observe ordinary rules of courtesy and good behavior.
6. Remember that this is not a victory for Negroes alone, but for all Montgomery and the South. Do not boast! Do not brag!
7. Be quiet but friendly; proud, but not arrogant; joyous, but not boisterous.
8. Be loving enough to absorb evil and understanding enough to turn an enemy into a friend.

Now for some specific suggestions:

1. The bus driver is in charge of the bus and has been instructed to obey the law. Assume that he will cooperate in helping you occupy any vacant seat.

2. Do not deliberately sit by a white person, unless there is no other seat.

3. In sitting down by a person, white or colored, say "May I" or "Pardon me" as you sit. This is a common courtesy.

4. If cursed, do not curse back. If pushed, do not push back. If struck, do not strike back, but evidence love and goodwill at all times.

5. In case of an incident, talk as little as possible, and always in a quiet tone. Do not get up from your seat! Report all serious incidents to the bus driver.

6. For the first few days try to get on the bus with a friend in whose non-violence you have confidence. You can uphold one another by glance or prayer.

7. If another person is being molested, do not arise to go to his defense, but pray for the oppressor and use moral and spiritual forces to carry on the struggle for justice.

8. According to your own ability and personality, do not be afraid to experiment with new and creative techniques for achieving reconciliation and social change.

9. If you feel you cannot take it, walk for another week or two. We have confidence in our people.

GOD BLESS YOU ALL.

THE MONTGOMERY IMPROVEMENT ASSOCIATION

The Rev. M. L. King, Jr., President

The Rev. W. J. Powell, Secretary

—*From* Inez Jessie Baskin Papers, *Alabama Department of Archives and History, Montgomery, Alabama. Available at http://www.alabamamoments.state.al.us/sec55ps.html*

1. Overall, how does the MIA suggest that blacks should act after the boycott victory? Why?

2. Which do you think is a more effective way to fight discrimination, staging protests such as the Montgomery boycott or taking cases to court?

Trouble at Central High: A Governor Defies the Law

In 1957 massive resistance met another challenge, this time in Little Rock, Arkansas, where the NAACP won a court order requiring the admission of nine black students to Central High School. When the "Little Rock Nine" tried to attend classes on September 23, riots broke out—not among the students, but among parents and other adults. Governor Orval Faubus brought in the state's National Guard. He did this not to protect the Little Rock Nine but to block them from entering the school. This brazen act of defiance forced the national government to take action. President Dwight Eisenhower federalized the state's National Guard, which required it to take orders from the federal government instead of Faubus. Eisenhower also sent U.S. Army troops, forcing the state to comply with the court order. Clearly *Brown* was only the first step in ending segregation in schools. In the following account, Melba Pattillo Beals, one of the Little Rock Nine, recalls September 25, 1957, when one thousand army paratroopers arrived to ensure the integration of Central High.

White students hold pro-segregation banners and photographs of Governor Orval Faubus in protest of the decision to allow black students to attend Little Rock's Central High. Although some students were vocal critics of the plan to integrate the school, most protesters were parents and other adults, often from communities outside of Little Rock.

AS WE NEARED THE SCHOOL, I could hear the roar of a helicopter directly overhead. . . . I could see that armed soldiers and jeeps had already blocked off certain intersections approaching the school. Closer to the school, we saw more soldiers and many more hostile white people with scowls on their faces, lining the sidewalk and shaking their fists. But for the first time I wasn't afraid of them.

We pulled up in front of the school. Groups of soldiers on guard were lined at intervals several feet apart. A group of twenty or more was running at breakneck speed up and down the street in front of

The National Guard, sent to Central High on the orders of President Eisenhower, safely escorts the Little Rock Nine to their classrooms. The protection afforded the black students some relief in their struggle to integrate the school, but the experience was a difficult one for Melba Pattillo and her eight peers.

Central High School, their rifles with bayonets pointed straight ahead. Sarge [the Little Rock Nine's army escort] said they were doing crowd control—keeping the mob away from us.

Sarge said we should wait in the station wagon because the soldiers would come for us. As I looked around, I saw a group of uniformed men walking toward us, their bayonets pointed straight up. . . . As I stepped outside the car, I heard a noise behind me. In the distance, there was that chillingly familiar but now muffled chant, "Two, four, six, eight. We ain't gonna integrate." . . .

Erect, rifles at their sides, their faces stern, the soldiers did not make eye contact as they surrounded us in a protective cocoon. After a long moment, the leader motioned us to move forward.

Hundreds of Central High students milled about. I could see their astonishment. Some were peering out of windows high above us, some were watching from the yard, others were on the landing. Some were tearful, others angry.

> "I felt proud and sad at the same time."

I felt proud and sad at the same time. Proud that I lived in a country that would go this far to bring justice to a Little Rock girl like me, but sad that they had to go to such great lengths. Yes, this is the United States, I thought to myself. There is a reason that I salute the flag. If these guys just go with us this first time, everything's going to be okay.

Step by step we climbed upward—where none of my people had ever before walked as a student. We stepped up to the front door of Central High School and crossed the threshold into that place where angry segregationist mobs had forbidden us to go.

—*From Melba Pattillo Beals,* Warriors Don't Cry: A Searing Memoir of the Battle to Integrate Little Rock's Central High. *New York: Pocket Books, 1994.*

THINK ABOUT THIS

1. Why was Melba no longer afraid of the angry mob waiting outside Central High?
2. From what Melba reported here, how do you think the white students at Central High felt about integration?

White Students Report Their Story: The Tiger

How did the average student at Central High feel about integration? Most of the students simply wanted their lives to get back to normal. As one student told the *New York Times,* "If the parents would just go home and leave us be we'd work this thing out for ourselves." One of the Little Rock Nine, Ernest Green, agreed: "Things would be better if only the grown-ups wouldn't mix in. The kids have nothing against us." Regardless of how the students felt, the adults could not be convinced. Governor Faubus closed Little Rock high schools at the end of the school year to prevent further integration, and they would remain closed throughout the 1958–1959 school year. Regardless of the governor's actions, the feelings of many Central High students are suggested by the following editorial, written by a student. It appeared in the school newspaper, *The Tiger,* shortly after the Little Rock Nine began attending Central High.

LET'S KEEP THE RECORD STRAIGHT

Just for the sake of the record, let us remind our readers that less than 1% of the population of Little Rock was in the crowd of people gathered in front of CHS when school opened Monday morning, September 23. In addition to that, many of the people in the crowd were not citizens of Little Rock. There was at no time any significant disturbance in the classrooms of the high school. From over the country there were a few photographers and reporters apparently seeking for a juicy morsel in the tense situation.

Again it is the case of where a minority group controlled the

"There was at no time any significant disturbance in the classrooms of the high school."

actions and even the thoughts of the majority. Wouldn't it be better for parents, townsmen, and strangers to let the law take its course and seek a remedy of the situation in some other way?

—From The Tiger *(Central High School student newspaper, Little Rock, Arkansas), October 3, 1957.*

THINK ABOUT THIS

1. According to the writer, who were the people who took part in the riots?
2. What point was the writer trying to make about civil disobedience in this editorial?

The Power of Peaceful Protest

THE NAACP AND THURGOOD MARSHALL used the court system in the fight for equality, but other civil rights activists looked to a different method: direct action. With the success of the Montgomery Bus Boycott, Martin Luther King Jr. had emerged as a powerful voice in the civil rights struggle. In 1957 he joined with other ministers and activists to found the Southern Christian Leadership Conference (SCLC). Its goal was to complement the NAACP's efforts with nonviolent, direct action— public protests such as boycotts and marches that were designed to bring about quick and effective change.

While studying to become a minister, King was introduced to the idea of peaceful protest as a means to fight oppression. He learned about Mahatma Gandhi, the great Indian leader who had opposed British rule of India through nonviolent resistance. As a result of Gandhi's efforts, India had achieved independence in 1947. King believed that Gandhi's technique represented the best path for black Americans. Soon the concept of nonviolence inspired activists around the country, especially in the South, where

Martin Luther King Jr. (center) during a press conference in Birmingham, Alabama. King became the face and voice of the civil rights movement—a powerful advocate of peaceful protest.

direct-action protests made significant strides. "You can struggle without hating," said King, "you can fight without violence."

Unfortunately, although most civil rights activists remained true to the principle of nonviolence, their opposition did not. Civil rights workers were jailed, beaten, humiliated, and even killed. But the dignity and honor of the civil rights movement, in the face of hostility, has left the people of the United States, especially black Americans, with a proud legacy.

King on Nonviolence

Gandhi's principles had been the guiding force behind the Montgomery Bus Boycott, and after its success, friends encouraged King to travel to India and witness firsthand the results of Gandhi's campaign. With his wife Coretta, King made the visit in 1959. It would solidify his commitment to nonviolence, making it the primary weapon in the battle for social change. In the following passage, King explains the concept of nonviolent protest.

"There is more power in socially organized masses on the march than there is in guns in the hands of a few."

THERE IS MORE POWER IN socially organized masses on the march than there is in guns in the hands of a few desperate men. Our enemies would prefer to deal with a small armed group rather than with a huge, unarmed but resolute mass of people. However, it is necessary that the mass action method be persistent and unyielding. Gandhi said the Indian people must

King successfully convinced most activists of the need to conduct themselves with dignity, but his adversaries held no such ideals. Civil rights protesters were attacked in any number of ways, as shown in this 1963 photograph in which police use high-pressure fire hoses to break up a demonstration.

"never let them rest," referring to the British. He urged them to keep protesting daily and weekly, in a variety of ways. This method inspired and organized the Indian masses and disorganized and demobilized the British. It educates its myriad participants, socially and morally. All history teaches us that like a turbulent ocean beating great cliffs into fragments of rock, the determined movement of people incessantly demanding their rights always disintegrates the old order.

—From Martin Luther King Jr., "The Social Organization of Non-Violence," Liberation, October 1959.

1. Why might an unarmed mass of resolute protesters be more effective than a small armed group?
2. What did King mean by "a turbulent ocean beating great cliffs"?

Students Take Action: The Greensboro Sit-In

On February 1, 1960, four black freshmen from the North Carolina Agricultural and Technical College sat down at an all-white lunch counter at the Greensboro Woolworth's. They politely asked to be served, but the waitress said, "We don't serve colored here." The young men waited, remaining seated at the counter until the store closed. The next day twenty more students joined them, and on the third day, white students from a local women's college took part in the protest as well. Soon the sit-ins spread across the state. Within two months students had staged sit-ins in fifty-four cities in nine states, at a variety of public places. All the while, the students obeyed a few simple rules, drawn up by a theology student named James Lawson: "Do show yourself friendly on the counter at all times. Do sit straight and face the counter. Don't strike back or curse back if attacked. Don't laugh out. Don't hold conversations. Don't block entrances." Segregationists assaulted the student protesters; sometimes people threw food or insulted them; other times, they pulled the students from their chairs, arrested them, or even attacked them with tear gas and police dogs. Still, the students knew that if they stayed true to the principle of nonviolence, no one could rightfully criticize them. The sit-ins set in motion a new

Pro-segregationists often provoked sit-in participants, hoping they would lose their composure and strike back. But a protest could be successful only if demonstrators refused to react.

phase in the civil rights movement, a phase in which students—both black and white—would play a major role. Later that year, the students who had participated in the sit-ins formed the Student Nonviolent Coordinating Committee (SNCC) to help organize more direct-action protests and involve people in the movement at the local level. Following is a letter from the leaders of the Greensboro sit-in, written to the president of Woolworth's.

WE THE UNDERSTATED ARE STUDENTS at the Negro college in the city of Greensboro. Time and time again we have gone into Woolworth stores of Greensboro. We have bought thousands of items at hundreds of the counters in your stores. Our money was accepted without rancor or discrimination and with politeness toward us, when at a long counter just three feet away our money is not acceptable because of the color of our skins. This letter is not being written with resentment toward your company, but with the hope of understanding. . . .

"Our money was accepted without rancor or discrimination."

We are asking that your company take a firm stand to eliminate discrimination. We firmly believe that God will give courage and guidance in the solving of this problem.

—*From Ezell Blair Jr., David Price, Joseph McNeil, David Richmond, and Franklin McCain (sit-in leaders), to the president of F. W. Woolworth & Company, letter of February 1, 1960. In Miles Wolff,* Lunch at the Five and Ten: The Greensboro Sit-Ins. *New York: Stein and Day, 1970.*

THINK ABOUT THIS

1. Why do you think blacks were permitted to purchase items at Woolworth's yet not eat at the lunch counter?
2. Why did protest leaders set rules for the students to follow at the sit-ins?

Freedom Ride: John Lewis Tells His Story

In 1960 the Supreme Court ruled that it was illegal to segregate modes of public transportation that traveled between states. This ruling included ticket counters, waiting rooms, and restaurants in train and bus stations. Not surprisingly, Southern states didn't comply. Leaders from the Congress of Racial Equality (CORE), an interracial civil rights organization, decided to protest continued segregation on buses. In the spring of 1961 twelve CORE members—black and white, male and female—took a "Freedom Ride" from Washington, D.C., to New Orleans. Divided into two groups and traveling on separate buses, they purchased their tickets in Washington without incident. But the farther south they traveled, the more intense the Freedom Ride became. In the following account John Lewis, the youngest of the twelve Freedom Riders, explains what happened when they reached Rock Hill, South Carolina. Lewis went on to become chairman of the SNCC, to organize voter registration drives, and, in 1986, to win a seat in the U.S. House of Representatives.

AS AL BIGELOW AND I APPROACHED the "white" waiting room in the Rock Hill Greyhound terminal, I noticed a large number of white guys hanging around the pinball machines in the lobby. Two of these guys were leaning by the doorjamb to the waiting room. They wore leather jackets, had those ducktail haircuts and were each smoking a cigarette.

"Other side, nigger," one of the two said, stepping in my way as I began to walk through the door. He pointed to a door down the way with a sign that said "colored."

A black woman is directed out of a waiting room for white passengers at a Texas bus station—precisely the kind of discrimination the Freedom Riders sought to challenge.

I did not feel nervous at all. I really did not feel afraid.

"I have a right to go in here," I said, speaking carefully and clearly, "on the grounds of the Supreme Court decision in the *Boynton* case."

I don't think either of these guys had ever heard of the *Boynton* case. Not that it would have mattered. . . .

The next thing I knew, a fist smashed the right side of my head. Then another hit me square in the face. As I fell to the floor I could feel feet kicking me hard in the sides. I could taste blood in my mouth.

At that point Al Bigelow stepped in, placing his body between mine and these men, standing square, with his arms at his sides.

It had to look strange to these guys to see a big, strong white man putting himself in the middle of a fistfight like this, not looking at all as if he was ready to throw a punch, but not looking frightened either.

They hesitated for an instant. Then they attacked Bigelow, who did not raise a finger as these young men began punching him. It took several blows to drop him to one knee.

At that point several of the white guys by the pinball machines moved over to join in. Genevieve Hughes [a white Freedom Rider] stepped in their way and was knocked to the floor.

That finally brought a reaction from a police officer who had stood by and witnessed the entire scene. He stepped in, pulled one guy off us and said, "All right boys. Y'all've done about enough now. Get on home."

Within minutes more police arrived, including a sympathetic officer who asked if we wanted to press charges. I was back on my feet by then, woozy and feeling stabs of sharp pain above both eyes and in my ribs. My lower lip was bleeding pretty heavily. . . .

We said no to the offer to press charges. This was simply another aspect of the Gandhian perspective. Our struggle was not against one person or against a small group of people like those who attacked us that morning. The struggle was against a *system,* the system that helped produce people like that. . . .

The attack that day—the first time blood was drawn on the Freedom Ride—did exactly what we wanted it to do. It drew attention.

—*From John Lewis,* Walking with the Wind:
A Memoir of the Movement. *New York: Simon and Schuster, 1998.*

THINK ABOUT THIS

1. Why didn't the Freedom Riders press charges against the attackers?
2. Why did the Freedom Riders want to attract attention?
3. Can you imagine the sort of courage it took to stand passively, without any attempt at self-defense, while being attacked?

Never at Ole Miss: Integrating the University of Mississippi

In 1962 a young man named James Meredith hoped to transfer from an African-American college and spend his senior year at "Ole Miss," the all-white University of Mississippi in the town of Oxford. Predictably, when he applied, the school resisted, enjoying the support of the state's highest officials—including Governor Ross Barnett, a zealous segregationist. When Meredith tried to register for classes in September 1962, Governor Barnett left the state capital for Oxford. He wanted to be the one to deny Meredith entrance to the school. "No school will be integrated in Mississippi while I'm governor," Barnett promised. As had happened a few years earlier in Little Rock, the federal government and the U.S. president—this time, John F. Kennedy—had to step in. Barnett was told that if he did not let Meredith into the school, he would be arrested. Following is his statement to the people of Mississippi on September 30, the day before Meredith arrived at the Ole Miss campus.

AS THE GOVERNOR OF THE STATE OF MISSISSIPPI, I have just been informed by the Attorney General of the United States that Meredith today has been placed on the campus of the University of Mississippi by means of government helicopters and is accompanied by federal officers.

I urge all Mississippians and instruct every state officer under my command to do everything in their power to preserve peace and to avoid violence in any form. Surrounded on all sides by the armed forces and oppressive power of the United States of America, my courage and my convictions do not waver. My heart still says, "Never," but my calm judgment abhors the bloodshed that would follow. I love Mississippi. I love her people. I love those ten thousand good Mississippians in the National Guard who have now been federalized and requested to oppose me and their people. I know that our principles remain true, but we must at all odds preserve the peace and avoid bloodshed.

"My heart still says, 'Never.'"

To the officials of the federal government, I say: Gentlemen, you are tramping on the sovereignty of this great state and depriving it of every vestige of honor and respect as a member of the Union of states. You are destroying the Constitution of this great nation. May God have mercy on your souls.

—From Governor Ross Barnett, to the people of Mississippi, broadcast September 30, 1962. Published in the Christian Science Monitor, October 1, 1962.

THINK ABOUT THIS

1. What did Barnett mean when he said that the National Guard had been federalized? Who had the power to federalize it?
2. What did Barnett say to show that he had not changed his views and only obeyed the law under force?
3. Barnett said that the federal government was destroying the Constitution by forcing a state school to accept James Meredith. Could he support this statement? How might someone argue against it?

James Meredith at Ole Miss

Angry crowds gathered the night of September 30, 1962, when Meredith arrived at Ole Miss escorted by federal marshals. Soon a

James Meredith, escorted by federal marshals, prepares to attend his first day of classes at Ole Miss.

mob of 2,500, most of whom were not students at the university, were yelling slurs across the campus. Bottles and bricks flew through the air, and gunshots were fired. By the end of the night, two people were dead, another shot in the throat. Hundreds more were injured before federal troops drove off rioters at five the next morning. Some five hundred troops patrolled the campus for the next eight months as Meredith completed his first year at Ole Miss. He graduated from the school on August 18, 1963, with a bachelor's degree in political science. At the graduation ceremony he wore— upside down—one of Barnett's old campaign pins. The pin said, "Never, Never." Time and again these were the words Barnett had spoken as he ran for office, promising the people of Mississippi that the state would never abolish segregation. He was wrong. Following is a statement by James Meredith about what it was like to attend Ole Miss during the first months after the crisis.

AS FAR AS MY RELATIONS WITH the students go, I make it a practice to be courteous. I don't force myself on them, but that's not my nature anyway. Many of them—most I'd say—have been courteous, and the faculty members certainly have been. When I hear the jeers and the catcalls . . . I don't consider it personal. I get the idea people are just having a little fun. I think it's tragic that they have to have this kind of fun about me, but many of them are children of the men who lead Mississippi today, and I wouldn't expect them to act any other way. . . .

"I don't consider it personal."

It hasn't been all bad. Many students have spoken to me pleasantly. They have stopped banging doors and throwing bottles into my dormitory now.

One fellow from my hometown sat down at my table in the cafeteria. "If you're here to get an education, I'm for you," he said. "If you're here to cause trouble, I'm against you." That seemed fair enough to me.

—From James Meredith, *"I'll Know Victory or Defeat,"* Saturday Evening Post, *November 10, 1962.*

THINK ABOUT THIS

1. Overall, do you think Meredith's experience at Ole Miss was positive?
2. Assume that the African-American schools actually were equal. Would there still have been a reason to desegregate white schools?

In the spring of 1963, the police chief of Birmingham, Alabama, announced an ordinance outlawing further civil rights demonstrations. The protesters would not give up, however, and many, like this seventeen-year-old boy, paid a price for their participation.

Chapter 6

In the Face of Violence

NOWHERE WAS AMERICAN RACISM MORE EVIDENT than in the Deep South, most notably in the states of Mississippi and Alabama. Martin Luther King called Birmingham, Alabama, the most segregated city in America, and there was hard evidence to back his claim. In 1960 *New York Times* reporter Harrison Salisbury visited the city to investigate its race relations: "Whites and blacks still walk the same streets," he wrote. "But the streets, the water supply and the sewer system are about the only public facilities they share." Birmingham was also the nation's most racially violent city. Salisbury told how racism and segregation were "reinforced by the whip, the razor, the gun, the bomb, the torch, the club, the knife, the mob, the police, and many branches of the state's apparatus."

The town's police chief, Eugene "Bull" Connor, was infamous for his strict segregationist beliefs. He commanded his men to break up all black political meetings and punished whites who were friendly to blacks. The manager of the city's bus terminal had been arrested twice for complying with orders to desegregate. It was

Eugene "Bull" Connor at a Birmingham demonstration

in Birmingham that Martin Luther King would launch his next campaign.

King, Ralph Abernathy, and other leaders from the SCLC began communicating with members of Birmingham's black community, who trained citizens in the techniques of nonviolence. At the invitation of Fred Shuttlesworth, the city's leading civil rights activist, King and other SCLC leaders arrived in Birmingham on April 2, 1963, to initiate Project C (for *Confrontation*). First they issued a statement demanding an immediate end to racial restrictions in all public places—from lunch counters to restrooms, stores to theaters. They called for an end to unfair hiring practices and for the formation of a committee to work toward total desegregation.

With the statement out, it was time to go to work. Protesters staged sit-ins at lunch counters; Bull Connor arrested 150 of them. A few days later 30 blacks marched on city hall; they, too, were arrested and sent to jail. The following day, Palm Sunday, police used dogs and nightsticks to break up a prayer march through downtown Birmingham. Connor secured a court order prohibiting civil rights activists from further protests, but demonstrations continued.

The events that took place in Birmingham in the spring of 1963 ignited civil rights demonstrations throughout the South. More than 100,000 Americans would participate in protests in the coming months. The civil rights movement had gained the nation's attention—and the world's as well.

Letter from a Birmingham Jail

With Bull Connor's court order in force, Martin Luther King had a choice to make. To continue demonstrations in Birmingham, he would have to defy the law. Yet the law was exactly what he was trying to uphold through peaceful protest. But as King told reporters, the protests in Birmingham had "reached the point of no return." On Good Friday he led some fifty marchers toward city hall, singing hymns along the way; a thousand black citizens stood by in support. Connor was furious; he ordered his squad with its snarling police dogs to arrest the demonstrators. Cameras and news reporters captured the event on film, and the nation watched police load King into a windowless police van. The next day several of the town's white clergymen took out an advertisement in the *Birmingham News,* saying the protests were "unwise and untimely."

"We do not believe that these days of new hope are days when extreme measures are justified in Birmingham," the clergymen wrote. King responded from jail, writing in the margins of a newspaper and on toilet paper. His response explained why the struggle against racism could not wait: "For years now, I have heard the word 'Wait.' It rings in the ears of every Negro with piercing familiarity. This 'Wait' has almost always meant 'Never.'" Following is more of King's powerful essay.

PERHAPS IT IS EASY FOR THOSE who have never felt the stinging dart of segregation to say, "Wait." But when you have seen vicious mobs lynch your mothers and fathers at will and drown your sisters and brothers at whim; when you have seen hate-filled policemen curse, kick and even kill your black brothers and sisters; when you see the vast majority of your twenty million Negro brothers smothering in an airtight cage of poverty in the midst of an affluent society; when you suddenly find your tongue twisted and your speech stammering as you seek to explain to your six-year-old daughter why she can't go to the public amusement park that has just been advertised on television, and see tears welling up in her eyes when she is told that Funtown is closed to colored children, and see ominous clouds of inferiority beginning to form in her little mental sky, and see her beginning to distort her personality by developing an unconscious bitterness toward white people; when you have to concoct an answer for a five-year-old son who is asking: "Daddy, why do white people treat colored people so mean?"; when you take a cross-country drive and find it necessary to sleep night after night in the uncomfortable corners of your automobile because no motel will accept you; when you are humiliated day in and day out by nagging signs reading "white" and "colored"; when your first name becomes "nigger," your middle name becomes "boy" (however old you are) and your last name becomes "John," and your wife and mother are never given the respected title "Mrs."; when you are harried by day and haunted by night by the fact that you are a Negro, living constantly at tiptoe

King's experience in Birmingham was not the first time he faced jail time for organizing direct action protests. Shown here with Ralph Abernathy (*center*), King was sent to prison in Montgomery during the bus boycott of 1956.

stance, never quite knowing what to expect next, and are plagued with inner fears and outer resentments; when you are forever fighting a degenerating sense of "nobodiness" then you will understand why we find it difficult to wait. There comes a time when the cup of endurance runs over, and men are no longer willing to be plunged into the abyss of despair. I hope, sirs, you can understand our legitimate and unavoidable impatience.

You express a great deal of anxiety over our willingness to break laws. This is certainly a legitimate concern. Since we so diligently urge people to obey the Supreme Court's decision of 1954 outlawing segregation in the public schools, at first glance it may seem rather paradoxical for us consciously to break laws. One may well ask: "How can you advocate breaking some laws and obeying others?" The answer lies in the fact that there are two types of laws: just and unjust. I would be the first to advocate obeying just laws. One has not only a legal but a moral responsibility to obey just laws. Conversely, one has a moral responsibility to disobey unjust laws. I would agree with St. Augustine that "an unjust law is no law at all."

Now, what is the difference between the two? How does one determine whether a law is just or unjust? A just law is a man-made code that squares with the moral law or the law of God. An unjust law is a code that is out of harmony with the moral law. To put it in the terms of St. Thomas Aquinas: An unjust law is a human law that is not rooted in eternal law and natural law. Any law that uplifts human personality is just. Any law that degrades human personality is unjust. All segregation statutes are unjust because segregation distorts the soul and damages the personality. It gives the segregator a false sense of superiority and the segregated a false sense of inferiority. Segregation, to use the terminology of the Jewish philosopher Martin Buber, substitutes an "I-it" relationship for an "I-thou" relationship and ends up relegating persons to the status of things. Hence segregation is not only politically, economically and sociologically unsound, it is morally wrong and sinful. Paul Tillich said that sin is separation. Is not segregation an existential expression of man's tragic separation, his awful estrangement, his terrible sinfulness? Thus it is that I can urge men to obey the 1954 decision of the Supreme Court, for it is morally right; and I can urge them to disobey segregation ordinances, for they are morally wrong.

> "... one has a moral responsibility to disobey unjust laws."

—From Martin Luther King Jr., "Letter from a Birmingham Jail."
April 16, 1963. Available online from the Martin Luther King Jr. Papers Project,
http://www.stanford.edu/group/King/popular_requests/

1. Give an example of another time that black activists were cautioned to be patient and wait for things to get better.
2. Explain how King justified breaking the law in protest.

The Children's Crusade: A Peaceful Protest Takes a Violent Turn

When King was freed on bail, he saw that the demonstrations were losing support. Many of the city's black citizens were in jail; those who weren't feared arrest or worse. Black businessmen complained of losing business; black religious leaders called for caution. With few adults eager to protest, SCLC leaders decided to enlist children in the cause. On May 2, 1963, more than a thousand children, aged six to eighteen years, marched in the streets of Birmingham, singing hymns and chanting freedom slogans. Bull Connor was unmoved; he summoned school buses to haul 950 of the children to jail. A thousand more students assembled the next day. Connor called in police dogs and firefighters to attack the terrified crowd. The firefighters aimed hoses at the children; water streamed at pressures high enough to remove bark from a tree. It ripped clothes and threw children to the ground and over parked cars. It drew blood. Television cameras recorded the confrontation. Around the nation, Americans watched in outrage as snarling dogs lunged at children. Viewers saw human beings hurled against walls by the powerful blast of a fire hose. They witnessed police attacking demonstrators with nightsticks. Horrified, leaders in Washington, D.C., knew they had to act. The Justice Department sent the assistant attorney general to negotiate peace between protesters and the

As more Americans witnessed violent incidents, such as the brutal attacks on young people participating in the Birmingham Children's Crusade, it was increasingly clear that the nation's leaders would have to find ways to better protect its citizens.

city. Knowing the protests would continue and the economy would suffer, the city eventually agreed. Following is a portion of the statement released by Shuttlesworth, King, and Abernathy describing the agreement made with the city of Birmingham.

RESPONSIBLE LEADERS OF BOTH Negro and white communities of Birmingham, being desirous of promoting conditions which will ensure sound moral, economic and political growth of their city, in the interest of all citizens of Birmingham, after mutual consideration and discussion of the issues relating to the recent demonstrations in the city, have agreed to the following:

1. The desegregation of lunch counters, rest rooms, fitting rooms, and drinking fountains, in planned stages within the next ninety days.

2. The upgrading and hiring of Negroes on a nondiscriminatory basis throughout . . . Birmingham. This will include the hiring of Negroes as clerks and salesmen within the next sixty days. . . .

3. Our movement has made arrangements for the release of all persons on bond or their personal recognizance. Our legal department is working with further solutions to this problem.

4. Through the Senior Citizens Committee or the Chamber of Commerce, communications between Negro and white to be publicly re-established within the next two weeks [in order to] prevent the necessity of further protest demonstrations.

—From Fred L. Shuttlesworth, Martin Luther King Jr., and Ralph Abernathy, joint statement of May 10, 1963. Published in the New York Times, May 11, 1963.

THINK ABOUT THIS

1. Can the terms of this agreement be considered a victory for the SCLC and the protesters?

2. Do you agree with the terms of the agreement? Should the protesters have demanded anything else?

A President's Promise

After the election of President Kennedy in 1960, civil rights supporters, both black and white, gained a new sense of hope. Kennedy had actively sought the black vote, and his youth and vigor held the promise of great change. But at the beginning of his term, Kennedy became all too familiar with the powerful presence of Southern leaders in Congress who blocked any attempt at civil rights legislation. At the same time, it was a critical moment in U.S. history. Cold War tensions were at an all-time high, and the nation sat poised at the edge of war with the Soviet Union. Kennedy had little time to focus on civil rights issues, but the alarming events in Birmingham changed this. Following is Kennedy's "Report to the American People on Civil Rights" of June 11, 1963, about one month following the agreement in Birmingham.

WE PREACH FREEDOM AROUND THE WORLD, and we mean it, and we cherish our freedom here at home, but are we to say to the world, and much more importantly, to each other that this is the land of the free except for the Negroes; that we have no second-class citizens except Negroes; that we have no class or caste system, no ghettoes, no master race except with respect to Negroes?

Now the time has come for this Nation to fulfill its promise. The events in Birmingham and elsewhere have so increased the cries for equality that no city or State or legislative body can prudently choose to ignore them.

The fires of frustration and discord are burning in every city, North and South, where legal remedies are not at hand. Redress is sought in the streets, in demonstrations, parades, and protests which create tensions and threaten violence and threaten lives.

We face, therefore, a moral crisis as a country and as a people. It cannot be met by repressive police action. It cannot be left to increased demonstrations in the streets. It cannot be quieted by

"It ought to be possible, in short, for every American to enjoy the privileges of being American," said Kennedy in his address to the nation. "But this is not the case."

token moves or talk. It is time to act in the Congress, in your State and local legislative body and, above all, in all of our daily lives.

It is not enough to pin the blame on others, to say this is a problem of one section of the country or another, or deplore the fact that we face. A great change is at hand, and our task, our obligation, is to make that revolution, that change, peaceful and constructive for all. . . .

I am, therefore, asking the Congress to enact legislation giving all Americans the right to be served in facilities which are open to the public—hotels, restaurants, theaters, retail stores, and similar establishments.

This seems to me to be an elementary right. Its denial is an arbitrary indignity that no American in 1963 should have to endure, but many do. . . .

I am also asking the Congress to authorize the Federal Government to participate more fully in lawsuits designed to end segregation in public education. . . .

But legislation . . . cannot solve this problem alone. It must be solved in the homes of every American in every community across our country. . . .

This is one country. It has become one country because all of us and all the people who came here had an equal chance to develop their talents.

We cannot say to 10 percent of the population that you can't have that right; that your children cannot have the chance to develop whatever talents they have; that the only way that they are going to get their rights is to go into the streets and demonstrate. I think we owe them and we owe ourselves a better country than that.

—From "Report to the American People on Civil Rights,"
President John F. Kennedy, The White House, June 11, 1963. From the
John Fitzgerald Kennedy Library, Boston, Massachusetts.

THINK ABOUT THIS

1. According to Kennedy, were civil rights laws important? What did he believe they could achieve? What could they not achieve?
2. Do you think Kennedy supported the demonstrations and protests?
3. How could the problems Kennedy described "be solved in the homes of every American"?

A Man of Courage

Around midnight on June 11, 1963, the night President Kennedy gave his landmark civil rights speech, Medgar Evers was shot dead in his driveway in Jackson, Mississippi. Evers knew his life was in danger; it had been for nearly a decade. In 1954 the NAACP had decided to send representatives into the Deep South. For years the organization had practically given up hope in Mississippi; blacks in the state were afraid even to talk about the

NAACP. But in an effort to gain new members and renew its work where it was most needed, the NAACP selected activists such as Evers to set up new offices in Deep South cities. Evers had two main responsibilities: to recruit members and to investigate violence against blacks. Evers was effective, and his success drew attention; that attention made him a target of hate. In his travels around the state, he was followed, threatened, beaten, and mocked, but the attacks did not stop him. Following is an account from Evers's wife, Myrlie, about the night of his murder, an event that galvanized the civil rights movement—in the state of Mississippi and beyond.

"A shot rang out, loud and menacing."

MEDGAR HAD TOLD ME THAT PRESIDENT KENNEDY was speaking on civil rights that night, and I made a mental note of the time. We ate alone, the children and I. It had become a habit now to set only four places for supper. Medgar's chair stared at us, and the children, who had heard about the president's address to the nation, planned to watch it with me. There was something on later that they all wanted to see, and they begged to be allowed to wait up for Medgar to return home. . . .

When President Kennedy appeared, all three children fell silent, knowing despite their youth that he was going to be talking about them. . . .

It was a moving speech, the most direct and urgent appeal for racial justice any President of the United States had ever made. It moved me and gave me hope and made what Medgar was doing seem more important than ever before. I remember wondering what the white people of Mississippi were thinking. . . .

Myrlie Evers at the funeral of her husband, Medgar, June 1963

Darrell heard the car first. "Here comes Daddy."

We listened to the familiar sound of the car. I roused myself as the tires reached the gravel driveway, stretched, and then heard the car door close. . . .

A shot rang out, loud and menacing. The children, true to their training, sprawled on the floor. I knew in my heart what it must mean.

I flew to the door, praying to be wrong. I switched on the light. Medgar lay face down at the doorway, drenched with blood.

I screamed, went to him, calling his name.

There was another shot, much closer, and I dropped to my knees. Medgar didn't move.

The children were around me now, pleading with him. "Please, Daddy, please get up!"

—From Myrlie Evers, For Us, the Living. *Jackson, MS: Banner Books, University Press of Mississippi, 1967.*

THINK ABOUT THIS

Why did the NAACP send people such as Evers into the Deep South, knowing it would be dangerous? Why were these activists willing to go?

Anthem of the Movement

On August 28, 1963, some 250,000 Americans—people of all races and from across the nation—marched down the Mall in Washington, D.C., to gather at the Lincoln Memorial. It was the largest peacetime gathering in American history: the March on Washington for Jobs and Freedom. Though some, including President Kennedy, feared the day might end in violence, it was a peaceful celebration. On June 19, true to his promise, President Kennedy had introduced a civil rights bill into Congress. The sea of people that swelled before the Lincoln Memorial gathered in support of the bill, hoping that their sheer numbers would convince members of Congress to pass it. The marchers held placards telling of their dreams for a better future: "We March for Effective Civil Rights Laws Now!" "We Demand Voting Rights Now!" "If You're Not Against Discrimination, You're Not for Freedom!" A day filled with inspiration in song and words ended with one of the most memorable speeches in American history: Martin Luther King's "I Have a Dream." And the day ended in hope. The civil rights movement was making a difference. Following are lyrics to a song that became the anthem not only of that day, but of the civil rights movement itself.

WE SHALL OVERCOME

> We shall overcome, we shall overcome
> We shall overcome someday
> Oh deep in my heart, I do believe
> That we shall overcome someday

We'll walk hand in hand, we'll walk hand in hand
We'll walk hand in hand someday
Oh deep in my heart, I do believe
That we shall overcome someday

We shall live in peace, we shall live in peace
We shall live in peace someday
Oh deep in my heart, I do believe
That we shall overcome someday

We shall brothers be, we shall brothers be
We shall brothers be someday
Oh deep in my heart, I do believe
That we shall overcome someday

The truth shall make us free, truth shall make us free
The truth shall make us free someday
Oh deep in my heart, I do believe
That we shall overcome someday

We are not afraid, we are not afraid
We are not afraid today
Oh deep in my heart, I do believe
That we shall overcome someday

—"We Shall Overcome," Silphia Horton, Frank Hamilton, Guy Carawan,
and Pete Seeger. New York: Ludlow Music, 1963.

Think about This

What about this song relates to the principles and the ideas of the civil
rights movement?

Four Little Girls: A Bomb Explodes in Birmingham

Less than a month after the March on Washington, tragedy shattered the hope inspired by the landmark gathering. It was a Sunday morning in Birmingham, and Sunday school was in session. A powerful bomb exploded in the basement of the all-black Sixteenth Street Baptist Church, killing eleven-year-old Denise McNair and three fourteen-year-olds, Addie Mae Collins, Carole Robertson, and Cynthia Wesley. Scores of others at the church were injured. It was no accident that the bombing took place at the Sixteenth Street Baptist Church; this had been the staging ground for the Children's Crusade earlier that year. The incident spurred rioting in the city as citizens took to the streets. The following report from an Alabama newspaper details the events that took place after the bombing.

ALL BIRMINGHAM WAITED with taut nerves Sunday night for a possible major eruption of racial violence.

City police and state Troopers covered the city in an all out

Denise McNair   Carole Robertson   Addie Mae Collins   Cynthia Wesley

effort to hold the lid tight. Streets were almost deserted as citizens heeded Mayor Albert Boutwell's plea, "Please stay home tonight."

But at police headquarters reports of death and violence kept coming in late into the night.

A 16-year-old Negro boy was reported shot and killed by a policeman after a rock-throwing incident.

A white man was reported shot.

Another Negro boy was reported slain while riding a bicycle.

A firebomb was reported thrown at a Negro home on "Dynamite Hill," which got its name from previous racial troubles.

A larger fire was reported several minutes later on Fourth Avenue South, several blocks away.

A Negro was reported wildly firing a shotgun.

A newspaper photograph offers visual description of the damage caused by the bombing of the Sixteenth Street Baptist Church. Attesting to the force of the blast, all the windows were blown out of the building across the street.

Rocks were hurled at cars in various parts of the city.

Less than a block from City Hall, a police wagon stopped to pick up a Negro who was obviously drunk. He yelled wildly inside the wagon.

A clump of white men converged on the wagon until warned back by police.

"I wish I could have gotten hold of him," muttered a young white man as the wagon pulled off.

But inside the adjacent bus station whites and Negroes sat quietly side by side.

Across the street an elderly white man was commenting to a friend, "It's a helluva comeoff when they start bombing churches and killing innocent people."

"'Please stay home tonight.'"

Inside City Hall, before which stood scores of helmeted State Troopers, a wary Albert Boutwell commented to newsmen in a masterpiece of understatement.

"There is considerable excitement in our city."

He retired with other city officials to draw up an appeal for law and order.

—From Arthur Osgood, *"Racial Tension Mounts in Birmingham after Four Killed in Church Bombing,"* The Montgomery Advertiser, *September 16, 1963.*

THINK ABOUT THIS

Why do you think riots broke out following the church bombing? In what other ways could citizens have responded to the incident?

Chapter 7

We Shall Overcome

TOWARD THE END OF 1963, the spirit of hope and commitment that had been born at the March on Washington was all but lost. The final blow came with the terrible news of John F. Kennedy's assassination. Without him, wondered activists, would there be any hope of the civil rights bill becoming law? His successor, Lyndon B. Johnson, was from Texas, a Southern state that made no secret of its racist policies.

But on November 27, 1963, five days after Kennedy's death, President Johnson addressed Congress and the nation for the first time. He promised to pass the civil rights bill in Kennedy's memory. "Let us continue," he declared, promising that Kennedy's ideas "so nobly represented must and will be translated into effective action." Lyndon Johnson, a former member of Congress who was no stranger to the legislative process, used his know-how and talent to get the bill passed. Believing that no politician—no American—could ignore the issue of civil rights, he would accept no compromises; the bill was passed without changes. Black activism had changed the shape of American politics.

President Lyndon B. Johnson presents Martin Luther King with the pen used to sign the Civil Rights Act—a lasting reminder of the achievement to which King had dedicated his life.

The passage of the Civil Rights Act of 1964 did not mark the end of the movement, for there was still work to be done. For one thing, the act failed to address fully the right of black citizens to vote. Galvanized for action, activists set their sights on ensuring that African Americans would be able to cast their votes safely and participate in the democratic process, even in the Deep South.

Between 1961 and early 1964, half a million new black voters had been registered. This increase was due in large part to the efforts of the Voter Education Project, a joint effort of several civil rights organizations. One state, however, managed to resist the project completely: Mississippi. Only 5 percent of eligible blacks in Mississippi were registered to vote; some counties did not have a single black voter. Whites in the state claimed blacks simply didn't want to vote, but this clearly was not the case. To register, African Americans had to take tests; white government employees determined whether they had passed. Potential voters could be denied registration for neglecting to dot an "i" or cross a "t." Sometimes they could lose their jobs simply by attempting to register. Those still willing to take that risk were often threatened with violence.

To find a way to solve this problem, Mississippi's civil rights groups launched a campaign to register black voters; it became known as Freedom Summer. The campaign had four goals: to expand black voter registration in the state, to organize the Freedom Democratic Party that would challenge the whites-only Mississippi Democratic Party, to establish Freedom Schools to teach reading and math to black children, and to open community centers where blacks could obtain legal and medical assistance.

Congress Takes Action: The Civil Rights Act of 1964

On February 10, 1964, the House of Representatives passed the civil rights measure by 290 to 130 votes. Still, everyone knew the real battle would be in the Senate, where Southerners had killed nearly every piece of civil rights legislation. But with Johnson as an ally and the nation's desire to honor the memory of President Kennedy, civil rights leaders hit the Capitol with an impressive campaign to get the bill passed. The Senate listened. On June 19, one year from the day Kennedy had proposed the act, the Senate passed the most important piece of civil rights legislation in the nation's history. Following is a selection from President Johnson's address before signing the bill, on July 2, 1964.

This is a proud triumph. Yet those who founded our country knew that freedom would be secure only if each generation fought to renew and enlarge its meaning. . . .

We believe that all men are created equal. Yet many are denied equal treatment.

We believe that all men have certain unalienable rights. Yet many Americans do not enjoy those rights.

We believe that all men are entitled to the blessings of liberty. Yet millions are being deprived of those blessings—not because of their own failures, but because of the color of their skin.

The reasons are deeply imbedded in history and tradition and the nature of man. We can understand—without rancor or hatred—how this all happened.

But it cannot continue. Our Constitution, the foundation of our Republic, forbids it. The principles of our freedom forbid it. Morality forbids it. And the law I will sign tonight forbids it. . . .

The purpose of the law is simple.

It does not restrict the freedom of any American, so long as he respects the rights of others.

It does not give special treatment to any citizen.

It does say the only limit to a man's hope for happiness, and for the future of his children, shall be his own ability.

". . . the only limit to a man's hope for happiness, and for the future of his children, shall be his own ability."

It does say that . . . those who are equal before God shall now also be equal in the polling booths, in the classrooms, in the factories, and in hotels, restaurants, movie theaters, and other places that provide service to the public. . . .

We will achieve these goals because most Americans are law-abiding citizens who want to do what is right. . . .

So tonight I urge every public official, every religious leader, every business and professional man, every workingman, every house-wife—I urge every American—to join in this effort to bring justice and hope to all our people—and to bring peace to our land.

—*From* Public Papers of the Presidents of the United States: Lyndon B. Johnson, *1963–64. Volume II, entry 446, pp. 842–844. Washington, D.C. Government Printing Office, 1965. Available online from the Lyndon B. Johnson Presidential Library: http://www.lbjlib.utexas.edu/johnson/archives.hom/speeches.hom/640702.asp*

1. Johnson quoted the Declaration of Independence, saying that all men have "certain unalienable rights." Did the Founders believe these rights applied to everyone who lived in the United States?

2. Johnson said Americans should "understand—without rancor or hatred" how racism and discrimination came to be a part of life. How might civil rights activists have felt about this?

3. How did the Civil Rights Act of 1964 "renew and enlarge" the meaning of freedom?

Freedom Summer: Volunteers Take On Mississippi

In June 1964 student volunteers from across the nation prepared to move into Mississippi's black neighborhoods. It was the beginning of Freedom Summer. Most volunteers were in their early twenties; they came from well-off families and the nation's best colleges and universities. About eight hundred of them—most of them white— agreed to pay their own way for the summer, to live with black families, and to face the dangers that the project would inevitably involve.

White Mississippi reacted with rage to Freedom Summer; across the state police forces were fortified, and crosses were burned—the symbolic racist protest of the Ku Klux Klan. A project leader told the volunteers plainly of what they could expect: "I may be killed and you may be killed."

On June 20 the first group of student volunteers and other activists began the journey south from Ohio. The next day three members of the party disappeared. They would never be seen alive again, except by their murderers—members of the Mississippi Ku Klux Klan. When the activists' bodies were found in August, all three had been shot; the one black man among the three had been severely beaten. The disappearance of the men had cast a dark shadow on Freedom Summer, but few of the volunteers gave up. Following is an account from volunteer Les Johnson, describing the world he encountered in Mississippi during Freedom Summer. He describes what it was like to go door to door, trying to register black Mississippians to vote.

A student volunteer assists a woman as she registers to vote.

CANVASSING IS VERY trying, you walk a little dusty street, with incredibly broken down shacks. The people sitting on porches staring away into nowhere—the sweat running down your face! Little kids half-naked in raggy clothes *all* over the place—this is what you face with your little packet of "Freedom Forms." . . . The walls are inevitably covered with a funeral hall calendar, a portrait calendar of President Kennedy, old graduation pictures. Maybe a new cheap lamp from Fred's dollar store.

You meet an afraid, but sometimes eager, curious face—one which is used to . . . saying "Yes Sir" to everything a white man says. . . . You see their pain, the incredible years of suffering etched in their worn faces; and then, if you convince them to sign, you leave. You walk down the deteriorating steps to the dirt, to the next house . . . and start in on your sales pitch again, leaving behind something which has broken you a little more. Poverty in the abstract does nothing to you. When you wake up to it every morning, and come down through the streets of it, and see the same old man on the ground playing the accordion, the same man selling peaches out of a basket too heavy for his twisted body, the same children, a day older—day closer to those men—after this every day, poverty is a reality that is so outrageous you have to learn to . . . become jaded for the moment—or else be unable to function.

"You see their pain, the incredible years of suffering."

—*From Doug McAdam,* Freedom Summer. *New York: Oxford University Press, 1988.*

THINK ABOUT THIS

1. How do you think seeing firsthand the poverty among Mississippi's black residents affected the student volunteers? How might it have changed their perspective about the project?

2. What kind of people volunteered for Freedom Summer? Why did they choose to participate, knowing it would be dangerous?

"Is This America?" Fannie Lou Hamer at the National Convention

Perhaps the most important project of Freedom Summer was the Mississippi Freedom Democratic Party (MFDP), a direct challenge to the all-white regular Democratic Party in the state. In August 1964 the national Democratic Party would be holding its convention. Members of the MFDP wanted to send delegates to this event. They selected sixty-eight Mississippi citizens, only four of whom were white. To attend the national convention, the MFDP delegates would have to take the place of the all-white delegation from the Mississippi Democratic Party. Achieving this would be a tremendous challenge. With the support of important members from the national party, delegates from other states, and twenty-five members of the U.S. Congress, the MFDP had the chance to bring its case before a committee that would decide which delegates from Mississippi would win seats at the convention.

Fannie Lou Hamer is shown here on August 22, 1964, speaking before the committee that would determine whether the Mississippi Freedom Democratic Party would be permitted to attend the Democratic national convention.

Several witnesses spoke to the committee about the state's brutal history. Of all the speakers, the most affecting was Fannie Lou Hamer, who described losing her job on a plantation, where she had lived and worked for eighteen years, simply because she had tried to register to vote. Moved to tears, she explained what blacks in Mississippi risked if they attempted to exercise their constitutional rights. In the end, the MFDP delegates did not achieve what they had hoped, but the "freedom party" made the nation take notice. Following is a portion of Hamer's emotional speech, in which she describes what happened to her in June 1963 while working on a voter registration drive. She and the several other workers were arrested at the Winona, Mississippi, bus station for entering a "whites only" waiting room. While in police custody the workers were severely beaten. Hamer suffered injuries that troubled her for the rest of her life.

I WAS CARRIED TO THE COUNTY JAIL, and put in the booking room. . . . After I was placed in the cell I began to hear the sound of kicks and horrible screams, and I could hear somebody say, "Can you say, yes, sir, nigger? Can you say yes, sir?"

And they would say other horrible names.

She would say, "Yes, I can say yes, sir."

"So say it."

She says, "I don't know you well enough."

They beat her, I don't know how long, and after a while she began to pray, and asked God to have mercy on those people.

And it wasn't too long before three white men came to my cell. One of these men was a State Highway Patrolman and he asked me where I was from, and I told him Ruleville, he said, "We are going to check this."

And they left my cell and it wasn't too long before they came back. He said, "You are from Ruleville all right," and he used a curse word, and he said, "We are going to make you wish you was dead."

I was carried out of that cell into another cell where they had two Negro prisoners. The State Highway Patrolman ordered the first Negro to take the blackjack [a piece of metal wrapped with leather that is used as a weapon].

The first Negro prisoner ordered me, by orders from the State Highway Patrolman for me, to lay down on a bunk bed on my face. . . .

After the first Negro had beat until he was exhausted the State Highway Patrolman ordered the second Negro to take the blackjack.

The second Negro began to beat and I began to work my feet, and the State Highway Patrolman ordered the first Negro who had beat me to sit upon my feet. . . . I began to scream and one white man got up and began to beat my head and told me to hush.

"I question America."

One white man—since my dress had worked up high, walked over and pulled my dress down and he pulled my dress back, back up. . . .

All of this is on account of us wanting to register, to become first-class citizens, and if the Freedom Democratic Party is not seated now, I question America, is this America, the land of the free and the home of the brave where we have to sleep with our telephones off of the hooks because our lives be threatened daily because we want to live as decent human beings, in America?

—From Fannie Lou Hamer, "The Testimony of Fannie Lou Hamer at the
1964 Democratic Convention," July 22, 1964. Available online at
http://www.calvin.edu/academic/cas/programs/pauleyg/voices/alphabli.htm

THINK ABOUT THIS

1. What makes Hamer's speech effective?

2. What elements are most disturbing about Hamer's story?

The Ballot or the Bullet: The Radical Voice of Malcolm X

In the later years of the modern civil rights movement, a more radical voice emerged—the voice of Malcolm X. Unlike Martin Luther King, Malcolm X did not believe nonviolence was the answer to ending discrimination but thought that blacks must achieve equality "by any means necessary." Malcolm X was a member of the Nation of Islam (also known as the Black Muslims), a religious movement founded on the idea of black separatism. He firmly supported its principle that blacks and whites could never coexist peacefully. Blacks, he said, must have the power to determine their own future. By the mid-1960s many African Americans had grown disillusioned with the slow pace of change; some had begun to respond in kind when faced with violence. To dissatisfied African Americans, Malcolm X provided an alternative. After his assassination in February 1965, his ideas gained increasing prominence as more young activists began to take a militant approach to equal rights. Following is an excerpt from a 1964 speech by Malcolm X, given before an Ohio audience. It provides a very different perspective on civil rights. Keep in mind that Malcolm X lived in the North, in New York City, and he was speaking to a Northern audience.

THE QUESTION TONIGHT, as I understand it, is "The Negro Revolt, and Where Do We Go From Here?" or "What Next?" In my little humble way of understanding it, it points toward either the ballot or the bullet. . . .

Malcolm X's approach to civil rights was very different from Martin Luther King's. His ideas could be shocking and often seemed to condone violence. But in a nation increasingly torn apart by racism, the voice of Malcolm X was one that some activists were ready to hear.

1964 threatens to be the most explosive year America has ever witnessed. The most explosive year. Why? It's also a political year. It's the year when all of the white politicians will be back in the so-called Negro community jiving you and me for some votes. The year when all the white political crooks will be right back in your and my community with their false promises, building up our hopes for a letdown, with their trickery and their treachery, with their false promises which they don't intend to keep. As they nourish these dissatisfactions, it can only lead to one thing, an explosion; and now we have the type of black man on the scene in America today . . . who just doesn't intend to turn the other cheek any longer. . . .

[I]t's time now for you and me to become more politically mature and realize what the ballot is for; what we're supposed to get when we cast a ballot; and that if we don't cast a ballot, it's going to end up in a situation where we're going to have to cast a bullet. It's either a ballot or a bullet.

". . . we have the type of black man on the scene in America today . . . who just doesn't intend to turn the other cheek any longer."

—From Malcolm X, "The Ballot or the Bullet." Speech delivered April 3, 1964. Republished in George Breitman, editor, Malcolm X Speaks. New York: Grove Weidenfeld, 1965.

THINK ABOUT THIS

1. Explain in your own words what Malcolm X meant by "the ballot or the bullet."
2. What was Malcolm X urging his audience to do?
3. Could Malcolm X have given this speech in the South?

The Last Battleground: Bloody Sunday in Selma, Alabama

In January 1965 Martin Luther King and the SCLC began a series of protests in Selma, Alabama, to bring national attention to the issue of voting rights. They planned a fifty-mile march from Selma to Montgomery, where they would present Governor

George Wallace with a petition of grievances. Wallace said the march would not be tolerated and issued an order to prohibit it, but the protesters began the march as planned. Police cars lined their route. Approaching Edmund Pettus Bridge, the protesters saw state troopers waiting for them on the other side with gas masks, hard hats, and billy clubs. "You have two minutes to turn around and go back to your church," said the commander. Within a minute, he gave orders to attack: "Troops advance!" Following is a report from the *New York Times* describing what happened next.

THE TROOPERS RUSHED FORWARD, their blue uniforms and white helmets blurring into a flying wedge as they moved.

The wedge moved with such force that it seemed almost to pass over the waiting column instead of through it.

The first 10 or 20 Negroes were swept to the ground screaming, arms and legs flying and packs and bags went skittering across the grassy divider strip and on to the pavement on both sides.

Those still on their feet retreated.

The troopers continued pushing, using both the force of their bodies and the prodding of their nightsticks.

"The Negroes cried out as they crowded together for protection and the whites on the sideline whooped and cheered."

A cheer went up from the white spectators lining the south side of the highway. The mounted possemen spurred their horses and rode at a run into the retreating mass. The Negroes cried out as they crowded together for protection and the whites on the sideline whooped and cheered.

The Negroes paused in their retreat for perhaps a minute still screaming and huddling together. Suddenly there was a report, like a gunshot, and a gray cloud spewed over the troopers and the Negroes.

"Tear gas!" someone yelled.

The cloud began covering the highway. Newsmen, who were confined by four troopers to a corner 100 yards away, began to lose sight of the action. But before the cloud finally hid it all there were several seconds of unobstructed view. Fifteen or twenty nightsticks could be seen through the gas flailing at the heads of the marchers.

The Negroes broke and ran. . . . Troopers and possemen, mounted and unmounted, went after them. Several more tear gas bombs were set off. One report was heard that sounded different. A white civil rights worker said later that it was a shotgun blast. . . .

—From Roy Reed, "Alabama Police Use Gas and Clubs to Rout Negroes," New York Times, *March 7, 1965.*

THINK ABOUT THIS

The governor and other whites in Alabama believed that force against the protesters was the only way to keep blacks from gaining power. Was this strategy effective in the long run?

The Voting Rights Act: Free at Last?

Increasingly alarmed by the violence committed against innocent people, the nation reacted with outrage to the events in Selma. Within little more than a week President Johnson had sent a voting rights bill to Congress to eliminate all illegal barriers to the right to vote. "This time, on this issue," said Johnson, "there must be no delay, no hesitation, and no compromise with our purpose." Signed into law on August 6, 1965, the act prohibited election laws that denied or restricted the voting rights of minorities. Following is an excerpt from President Johnson's remarks prior to signing the act.

THIS LAW COVERS MANY PAGES. But the heart of the act is plain. Wherever, by clear and objective standards, States and counties are using regulations, or laws, or tests to deny the right to vote, then they will be struck down. If it is clear that State officials still intend to discriminate, then Federal examiners will be sent in to register all eligible voters. When the prospect of discrimination is gone, the examiners will be immediately withdrawn.

And, under this act, if any county anywhere in this Nation does not want Federal intervention it need only open its polling places to all of its people.

This good Congress, the 89th Congress, acted swiftly in passing this act. I intend to act with equal dispatch in enforcing this act.

And tomorrow at 1 P.M., the Attorney General has been directed to file a lawsuit challenging the constitutionality of the poll tax in the State of Mississippi. This will begin the legal process which, I confidently believe, will very soon prohibit any State from requiring the payment of money in order to exercise the right to vote. . . .

"You must register. You must vote."

And on that same day, next Tuesday, additional poll tax suits will be filed in the States of Texas, Alabama, and Virginia. . . .

Presidents and Congresses, laws and lawsuits can open the doors to the polling places and open the doors to the wondrous rewards which await the wise use of the ballot. . . .

But only the individual Negro, and all others who have been denied the right to vote, can really walk through those doors, and can use that right, and can transform the vote into an instrument of justice and fulfillment.

So, let me now say to every Negro in this country: You must register. You must vote. You must learn, so your choice advances your interest and the interest of our beloved Nation. Your future, and your children's future, depend upon it, and I don't believe that you are going to let them down.

If you do this, then you will find, as others have found before you, that the vote is the most powerful instrument ever devised by man for breaking down injustice and destroying the terrible walls which imprison men because they are different from other men.

—*From President Lyndon B. Johnson, Remarks in the Capitol Rotunda at the Signing of the Voting Rights Act, August 6, 1965.* Public Papers of the Presidents of the United States: Lyndon B. Johnson, 1965. *Volume II, entry 394. Washington, D.C.: Government Printing Office, 1966.*

THINK ABOUT THIS

1. Compare Johnson's words to the Malcolm X speech, "The Ballot or the Bullet." Are there any similarities?
2. Once the Voting Rights Act was passed and enforced, who would hold the responsibility for ensuring that black Americans voted?

"When we allow freedom to ring—when we let it ring from every village and every hamlet, from every state and every city, we will be able to speed up that day when all of God's children—black men and white men, Jews and Gentiles, Protestants and Catholics—will be able to join hands and sing in the words of the old Negro spiritual: 'Free at last! Free at last! Thank God Almighty, we are free at last!'" —*Martin Luther King Jr., 1963*

Epilogue

Legacy of a Movement

The passage of the Voting Rights Act is thought by many to mark the beginning of the end of the civil rights movement. Serious issues began to divide activists. Young members of the SNCC and CORE had begun to question the principle of nonviolence; some even objected to the participation of white people in an African-American struggle. As one young activist announced, "We don't need any more white phonies and liberals invading our movement." These strong feelings gave rise to the Black Power movement, which focused on blacks' self-reliance and racial dignity. In 1966 Huey Newton and Bobby Seale founded the Black Panther Party, an organization that believed self-defense was justified in all attempts to bring social and economic equality to the United States. The Panthers believed blacks had a right to defend themselves against police brutality and other forms of anti-black violence. Both Black Power supporters and the Panthers found inspiration in the work of Malcolm X.

Sadly, violence did become a part of the movement, especially in urban areas. Five days after the signing of the Voting Rights Act, a six-day riot broke out in Watts, a black neighborhood in Los Angeles. The following year would see even more chaos, as riots erupted in more than one hundred U.S. cities. President Johnson created a commission to study the outbreak of urban violence. The commission concluded that civil rights legislation had not done enough to help black America, warning that the nation "is moving toward two societies, one black and one white—separate and unequal."

More moderate activists also continued their work in the second half of the 1960s. Martin Luther King turned his attention to fighting poverty in the black community—not only in the South, but across the nation. In 1968 he planned another major protest, the Poor People's March, which would take place in Washington on April 28. The march did take place, but without its leader. On April 4, 1968, Martin Luther King was assassinated at a motel in Memphis, Tennessee. Within hours of the announcement of his death, violence raged in 130 cities across the country, leaving 46 people dead, 3,000 injured, and some 27,000 in jail. The peaceful civil rights movement had come to an end.

Did the movement achieve all that it could have? Certainly the legislation and court rulings made a great difference in the nation's future. Yet legislation wasn't enough; as Dwight Eisenhower said at the height of the Little Rock Nine crisis, "[Y]ou cannot change people's hearts merely by laws." But he went on to say that laws do express the conscience of a nation. In that way the civil rights movement made America see that too many of its people were denied the freedom promised by democracy. The movement could not change every American's heart, but it did begin the process. There is still so much further to go.

After the tumultuous presidential election of 2000, black voters in Florida accused election officials of denying them the right to vote—thirty-five years after the Voting Rights Act became law. There have also been charges of resegregation. Since the 1980s, blacks and whites in many areas have been attending separate schools again—not because of discrimination laws but because whites live in wealthier neighborhoods. In places where blacks and whites live close to each other, some white families have been choosing to send their children to private schools. And this trend has not been confined to the South; in 2002 the most segregated school districts in America were in New York State. Perhaps worst of all, lynching has not disappeared. In 1998 three Texas racists brutally beat James Byrd, chained him to the back of a pickup truck, and dragged him for several miles. They murdered James Byrd because he was black.

Today, at the dawn of a new millennium, the nation continues to struggle with racism. Today, some three decades after the March on Washington, Martin Luther King's words to the crowd gathered at the Lincoln Memorial continue to have meaning. And they continue to promise a brighter future.

I HAVE A DREAM that one day this nation will rise up and live out the true meaning of its creed: "We hold these truths to be self-evident, that all men are created equal."

I have a dream that one day on the red hills of Georgia the sons of former slaves and the sons of former slave owners will be able to sit down together at the table of brotherhood.

I have a dream that one day even the state of Mississippi, a state sweltering with the heat of injustice, sweltering with the heat of oppression, will be transformed into an oasis of freedom and justice.

I have a dream that my four little children will one day live in a nation where they will not be judged by the color of their skin but by the content of their character.

I have a dream today.

I have a dream that one day down in Alabama, with its vicious racists, with its governor having his lips dripping with the words of interposition and nullification—one day right there in Alabama little black boys and black girls will be able to join hands with little white boys and white girls as sisters and brothers.

I have a dream today.

I have a dream that one day every valley shall be exalted, and every hill and mountain shall be made low, the rough places will be made plain, and the crooked places will be made straight, and the glory of the Lord shall be revealed and all flesh shall see it together.

"I have a dream that my four little children will one day live in a nation where they will not be judged by the color of their skin but by the content of their character."

This is our hope. This is the faith that I go back to the South with. With this faith we will be able to hew out of the mountain of despair a stone of hope. With this faith we will be able to transform the jangling discords of our nation into a beautiful symphony of brotherhood. With this faith we will be able to work together, to pray together, to struggle together, to go to jail together, to stand up for freedom together, knowing that we will be free one day.

This will be the day, this will be the day when all of God's children will be able to sing with new meaning "My country 'tis of thee, sweet land of liberty, of thee I sing. Land where my fathers died, land of the Pilgrim's pride, from every mountainside, let freedom ring!"

And if America is to be a great nation, this must become true. And so let freedom ring from the prodigious hilltops of New Hampshire. Let freedom ring from the mighty mountains of New York. Let freedom ring from the heightening Alleghenies of Pennsylvania.

Let freedom ring from the snow-capped Rockies of Colorado. Let freedom ring from the curvaceous slopes of California.

But not only that; let freedom ring from Stone Mountain of Georgia.

Let freedom ring from Lookout Mountain of Tennessee.

Let freedom ring from every hill and molehill of Mississippi—from every mountainside.

Let freedom ring. And when this happens, and when we allow freedom to ring—when we let it ring from every village and every hamlet, from every state and every city, we will be able to speed up that day when all of God's children—black men and white men, Jews and Gentiles, Protestants and Catholics—will be able to join hands and sing in the words of the old Negro spiritual: "Free at last! Free at last! Thank God Almighty, we are free at last!"

—From Martin Luther King Jr., "I Have a Dream." Speech delivered at the March on Washington for Jobs and Freedom, August 28, 1963. Available online from the Martin Luther King Jr. Papers Project, http://www.stanford.edu/group/King/popular_requests/

Time Line

1865
Amendment XIII is passed.

1870
Amendment XV is passed.

1896
The Supreme Court rules against Homer Plessy, setting in motion the "separate but equal" doctrine and overturning the Civil Rights Act of 1875.

1890
Louisiana passes the Separate Car Activities statute.

1 8 0 0 s

1892
Homer Plessy is arrested for riding in a white train car in New Orleans.

1875
The first Civil Rights Act is passed.

W. E. B. Du Bois writes The Souls of Black Folk.
1903

1868
Amendment XIV is passed.

Ida B. Wells publishes A Red Record.
1895

1916

The NAACP establishes its Anti-Lynching Committee.

1939

Marian Anderson sings at the Lincoln Memorial on Easter Sunday.

President Harry Truman issues Executive Order 9981, which leads to the desegregation of the military.

1938

Charles Hamilton Houston successfully tries Gaines v. Registrar of the University of Missouri case before the Supreme Court.

1948

1909

The NAACP is founded.

1 9 0 0 s →

William Monroe Trotter meets with President Wilson at the White House and challenges the government's segregation policies.

1914

During Red Summer, at least twenty-five anti-black riots take place in cities all over the country.

1919

1942

Thurgood Marshall gives a speech explaining how the law can be used to fight discrimination.

1947

Jackie Robinson becomes the first black man to play major league baseball.

1956

The Supreme Court decides that segregated seating on public transportation is illegal. The Montgomery Bus Boycott ends after 381 days.

1954

In Brown v. the Board of Education, the U.S. Supreme Court decides that segregated schools are unconstitutional.

WAITING ROOM FOR WHITE ONLY

→

BY ORDER POLICE DEPT.

1 9 5 0 s

Martin Luther King and other activists form the Southern Christian Leadership Conference.

Emmett Till is murdered in Mississippi by two white men.

AUGUST 28, 1955

1957

Rosa Parks is arrested when she refuses to give up her seat to a white passenger on a Montgomery, Alabama, bus. The city's black community begins a boycott of public buses.

DECEMBER 1, 1955

Riots start when the Little Rock Nine attempt to attend Central High School in Little Rock, Arkansas.

SEPTEMBER 1957

FEBRUARY 1, 1960

Four black freshmen stage a sit-in at a Greensboro, North Carolina, lunch counter; hundreds of similar protests follow.

AUGUST 1964

The bodies of the missing Freedom Summer volunteers are found. Fannie Lou Hamer delivers a moving speech at the Democratic National Convention.

APRIL 1961

The SNCC is organized. The first Freedom Riders leave Washington, D.C.

1962

James Meredith attempts to enroll at the University of Mississippi.

FEBRUARY 21, 1965

Malcolm X is assassinated by former colleagues from the Nation of Islam.

MARCH 7, 1965

State troopers attack peaceful protesters at the beginning of a march from Selma to Montgomery.

AUGUST 6, 1965

Johnson signs the Voting Rights Act.

1966

The Black Panther Party is founded.

1 9 6 0 s

APRIL 2, 1963

Project C begins in Birmingham, Alabama, resulting in the arrest of Martin Luther King and other leaders.

JUNE 11, 1963

President Kennedy delivers his civil rights address. Near midnight, activist Medgar Evers is assassinated in Mississippi.

Some 250,000 people gather at the Mall in Washington, D.C., for the March on Washington for Jobs and Freedom.

AUGUST 28, 1963

Martin Luther King is assassinated.

APRIL 4, 1968

SCLC workers travel to Selma, Alabama, to begin protests for voting rights.

JANUARY 1965

The Civil Rights Act is signed.

JULY 2, 1964

SEPTEMBER 15, 1963

The bombing of the all-black Sixteenth Street Baptist Church in Birmingham, Alabama, ends in the deaths of four girls and scores of other injuries.

Glossary

activism participation in activities to bring attention to a cause

canvassing traveling through an area and meeting with people to gain political support or determine opinions about a given subject

caste a social division (or class) based on differences in wealth, profession, occupation, or race

civil having to do with the citizenry of a state or nation

constitutional abiding by the principles of the U.S. Constitution

delegate a representative to a convention or meeting

direct action actions, such as protests, strikes, and boycotts, designed to achieve a goal quickly

executive order an enactment by the president that does not require action from Congress

federalized made to serve the national government

integration incorporating people from different races or backgrounds into society as equals so that all people have equal access to facilities and services

legislation the laws that are made or passed by a lawmaking body such as Congress

minstrel shows theatrical performances in the nineteenth and early twentieth centuries in which whites wore black makeup to perform African-American song and dance; minstrel shows reinforced stereotypes and prejudices that white people held about blacks

National Guard citizens trained for immediate active duty in an emergency but otherwise held in reserve, or inactive duty

naturalize to make a citizen of someone who was born in another country

plaintiff a person who brings a case to court

Reconstruction the period following the Civil War, when Confederate states were reorganized into the Union

segregation the separation of a race, class, or other group by means of discriminatory laws and policies

sharecropper a tenant farmer who receives seed, tools, food, and living quarters, who works the land, and who receives an agreed share of the value of the crop minus charges; sharecroppers in the South generally were very poor

status quo the existing state of affairs

suffrage the right to vote

vigilante a member of a volunteer group that works to fight and punish crime without due process of law

To Find Out More

BOOKS

Archer, Jules. *They Had a Dream: The Civil Rights Struggle from Frederick Douglass to Marcus Garvey to Martin Luther King and Malcolm X.* New York: Puffin, 1996.

Davis, Townsend. *Weary Feet, Rested Souls.* New York: W. W. Norton, 1998.

King, Casey, et al. *Oh Freedom! Kids Talk about the Civil Rights Movement with the People Who Made It Happen.* New York: Knopf, 1997.

King, Martin Luther, Jr. *The Autobiography of Martin Luther King, Jr.* New York, Warner Books, 1998.

Lewis, John. *Walking with the Wind: A Memoir of the Movement.* New York: Simon & Schuster, 1999.

McKissack, Patricia, and Frederick McKissack. *The Civil Rights Movement in America: From 1865 to the Present.* 2nd ed. Chicago: Children's Press, 1991.

Mills, Kay. *This Little Light of Mine: The Life of Fannie Lou Hamer.* New York: Dutton, 1993.

Myers, Walter Dean. *Malcolm X: A Fire Burning Brightly.* New York: HarperCollins, 2000.

Shakoor, Jordana Y. *Civil Rights Childhood.* Jackson, MS: University Press of Mississippi, 1999.

Wexler, Sanford. *An Eyewitness History of the Civil Rights Movement.* New York: Checkmark Books, 1993.

WEB SITES

The Web sites listed here were in existence in 2003–2004 when this book was being written. Their names or locations may have changed since then.

In general, when using the Internet to do research on a history topic, you should use caution. You will find numerous Web sites that are very attractive to look at and appear to be professional in format. Proceed with caution, however.

Many, even the best ones, contain errors. Some Web sites even insert disclaimers or warnings about mistakes that may have made their way into the site. In the case of primary sources, the builders of the Web site often transcribe previously published material, good or bad, accurate or inaccurate. Therefore, you have to judge the content of *all* Web sites. This requires a critical eye.

A good rule for using the Internet as a resource is always to compare what you find in Web sites to several other sources such as librarian- or teacher-recommended reference works and major works of scholarship. By doing this, you will discover the myriad versions of history that exist.

Visit the Web site of the National Civil Rights Museum:
http://www.civilrightsmuseum.org/

For more information about the "separate but equal" rulings, visit the Constitutional Conflicts Web site:
http://www.law.umkc.edu/faculty/projects/ftrials/conlaw/ sepbutequal.htm

To learn more about the Little Rock Nine and Central High, visit the Little Rock Central High 40th Anniversary Web site:
http://www.centralhigh57.org/index.html

To learn more about African-American history, visit the African American Odyssey Web site of the Library of Congress:
http://memory.loc.gov/ammem/aaohtml/exhibit/aointro. html

To read oral histories of African Americans' stories of the civil rights movement, visit the University of Mississippi Civil Rights Documentation Project:
http://www-dept.usm.edu/~mcrohb/

Visit the Montgomery Bus Boycott Page, an excellent site for students:
http://socsci.colorado.edu/~jonesem/montgomery.html

For more primary sources of the civil rights struggle, visit:
http://occawlonline.pearsoned.com/bookbind/pubbooks/ nash5e_awl/medialib/timeline/docs/divdocs08.html

For more on the history of Jim Crow, visit:
http://www.jimcrowhistory.org/

Index

Page numbers for illustrations are in boldface

ABOUT THE AUTHOR

Elizabeth Sirimarco published her first book in 1990. Since that time she has written books for young people on subjects ranging from tennis to Thomas Jefferson, the Yanomami to Steven Spielberg. "The best thing about writing," she says, "is that I still have the chance to learn new things—it's like being in school again. Kids probably wouldn't understand—I wouldn't have believed it at their age—but I really miss school!"

A graduate of the University of Colorado at Boulder, Elizabeth also earned a degree in Italian from the Università per Stranieri in Siena, Italy. In addition to writing, she is an editor and occasionally enjoys the opportunity to work as an Italian translator. She and her husband, David, a photographer, live with their rottweiler and two cats in Denver, Colorado.